Beastie Boys

BEASTIE BOYS...IN THEIR OWN WORDS

Exclusive distributors:

Book Sales Limited
8-9 Frith Street, London W1V 5TZ, UK

Music Sales Corporation
257 Park Avenue South, New York, NY 10010, USA

Five Mile Press
22 Summit Road, Noble Park, Victoria 3174, Australia

Exclusive distributors to the music trade only:

Music Sales Limited
8-9 Frith Street, London W1V 5TZ, UK

ISBN 0.7119.7636.8
Order No. OP48132

Copyright © 1999 Omnibus Press
(A Division of Book Sales Limited)

A catalogue record for this book is available from the British Library

Compilation and introduction by Michael Heatley

All photographs supplied by LFI

Edited by Chris Charlesworth

Series design concept by Pearce Marchbank/Studio 20

Cover and Book designed and originated by Hilite

Picture research by Nikki Russell, Omnibus Press

Every effort has been made to trace the copyright holders of
the photographs in this book but one or two were unreachable.
We would be grateful if the photographers concerned would
contact us.

Printed in Great Britain by Page Bros Ltd, Norwich, Norfolk.

Visit Omnibus Press at
www.omnibuspress.com

OMNIBUS PRESS

If punk's *annus horribilis*, 1977, ensured the music business would never be the same again, then The Beastie Boys' chart-topping début album *Licensed To Ill* made sure the tenth anniversary was celebrated in style. Spending seven weeks at Number 1 on the *Billboard* pop chart, and – equally significantly – Number 2 on the black listing, it was the fastest-selling record in CBS Records' history.

The trio's groundbreaking combination of grinding heavy-metal riffs and gritty, street-style lyrics would have been impressive enough even without a hate campaign from the British tabloid press that rivalled the one levelled at the Sex Pistols a decade earlier. But the combination of the two put the Beasties

dramatically on the map. Questions were asked about the group in parliament, while Adam Horovitz was arrested for (supposedly) assaulting a member of the audience from the stage. Meanwhile, terrified Volkswagen owners slept in their cars for fear Beastie Boys fans would 'liberate' the metal bonnet badges as a 1980s alternative to the disco-era medallion… the group was indeed the talk of the town.

It had all begun back in 1981 when two young, loud and snotty New Yorkers, Mike Diamond (alias Mike D) and Adam Yauch (MCA), got together with drummer Kate Schellenbach and guitarist John Berry to open for bands such as the Misfits, plying their undemanding hardcore punk rock to a small but dedicated audience. Their first release, 'Pollywog Stew' on local indie label Ratcage Records, gave few clues as to what was to come.

Bizarrely, the group celebrated the release of their first record by breaking up (Schellenbach later resurfaced in Luscious Jackson, whom the Beasties signed to their label), and when they reformed in early 1983, Diamond and Yauch added Horovitz, alias Adrock (the son of playwright Israel Horovitz) to the ranks on guitar. The first recorded fruit of this new trio, 'Cookie Puss'/'Beastie Revolution', was designed to appeal to rap fans as much as their existing hardcore audience. A DJ was added to the line-up in the shape of Rick Rubin, who introduced them to high-flying manager Russell Simmons – and when the two formed Def Jam Records in 1984, the Beasties were the roster's first signings.

The equally significant patronage of teen queen Madonna, who chose The Beastie Boys to open the show on her *Like A Virgin Tour*, gave them a shortcut to notoriety, while the *Raising Hell Tour* in the summer of 1985 teaming them with Run DMC and LL Cool J, gave them the experience of playing large arenas to a predominantly black audience. Having staked a claim to two very different segments of the 1980s music audience, the début long-player, *Licensed To Ill*, joined the dots and revealed a most impressive picture.

A ruckus with Def Jam over royalties saw them switch label for *Paul's Boutique* – an album which, with sales of less than a million copies, would only later be acclaimed as an influence on the likes of Beck. It also launched the career of up-and-coming production team the Dust Brothers, who would work with the Rolling Stones a decade later.

The early 1990s found the Beasties straying from the spotlight, forming their own Grand Royal label and building their own studios as well as a clothing marque; Adam Horovitz also became a film star, of sorts. They regrouped for *Check Your Head*, recorded in 1992 with keyboardist Money Mark, which mixed funk, hip-hop and even a touch of punk to admirable effect.

Its Top 10 success gave them college cred and allowed *Ill Communication* to début at Number 1 two years later. Headliners on the annual *Lollapalooza* tour, the group had slickly metamorphosed from white rappers to stalwarts of the alternative rock scene. *Hello Nasty*, released in 1998, confirmed the most effective comeback since Lazarus and assured the world that, over a decade on from their headline-grabbing heyday, The Beastie Boys were still a force to be reckoned with.

Regardless of commercial standing, The Beastie Boys have never been anything less than quotable. And their worldview expanded significantly in 1994 when, having sampled local musicians for several songs on *Ill Communication*, they repaid the compliment by forming a non-profit organisation, the Milarepa Fund, to raise money for (and awareness of the plight of) the Tibetan people, as well as staging benefit concerts. And in 1998 they engaged in a spat with shock-rave-rockers the Prodigy over the lyric of 'Smack My Bitch Up' – the Beasties having long since renounced the seemingly sexist stance of their early days.

The Beastie Boys have evolved from a headline-grabbing novelty act into one of the most popular and influential bands of the 1990s; one can only speculate as to their potential impact on the forthcoming millennium. Their musical direction and opinions may have mellowed over time, but they've never been anything less than opinionated.

Time to get ill...

Beasts in Short Pants

The early days

We came together in 1979, it says so right here in the record-company biography. When we started we had a different guitarist and a different drummer. We were a hardcore (heavy metal) group. I was playing the bass and Michael (Mike D) was the singer.

Then the guitarist left, and Adam had another group. We were hanging out a lot, and he became the guitarist in our group.
Adam Y, 1986

Nobody ever asked me to join. I just did.
Adam H, September 1998

I was this incredibly awkward punk-rock kid with spiky hair. I'd tried to dye it orange but it hadn't really worked at all and it looked like shit. I was going to a lot of punk rock shows on my own because I didn't have any friends at school who were into that. And because I was young and (Adam Yauch) was young, a lot younger than most people at the gigs, we became part of this group of kids who went to clubs to see bands together.

I don't know if it's to do with being from New York or just from being insecure, but we certainly didn't stroll up to each other and say, 'What's up?' We scowled at each other for some time first.
Mike D, July 1998

I recognised them from all over the place. I first saw Yauch at the Rat Cage, this record shop people used to hang out in. We'd cut school and hang out there.
Adam H, September 1998

It was a relief to find other people who were into punk rock and felt the same way I did. All the other kids at school were jerks as far as we were concerned because they weren't into Black Flag. They were actually crucial in turning us on to the idea that we could make music because previously many of the groups we liked were British, but Black Flag were American. It made the idea of being in a band less remote.
Mike D, July 1998

When we first started, a lot of people, not people in the music business – a lot of rappers and DJs have always taken us seriously – but to a lot of people it was just inconceivable for white kids to be rapping. It was like we'd suddenly decided to become American Indians for a while and live on the reservation.

Now we've been doing it for a while we've built up some respect. We definitely broke some ground, but we definitely went through some embarrassing gigs doing it.
Adam Y, January 1987

My father is a totally self-made man who grew up from nothing in the Bronx and moved to Manhattan through his own wits. The idea to me that you would want to grow up to just work for someone else, and that you'd forge a happy life that way was never a consideration.
Mike D, November 1997

Why did we decide to use Internal Excellence as the last two letters in Beastie (Boys Entering Anarchistic States Towards Internal Excellence)? I don't know. It was just a goof at the time when we were forming the band. We were just trying to think of the stupidest things we possibly could and it seemed funny. In retrospect it surprises me that it's come to make sense. I like that.
Adam Y, 1997 , on The Beastie Boys name.

The name was more like a goof on the Angry Samoans. It was me and (original guitarist) John Berry sitting around in my room in Brooklyn, just kickin' around names. It was Beastie this, or Boys that. And we just said 'Let's go with that one – it sounds pretty stupid, like some Angry Samoans hardcore shit.' Then we started making buttons (badges) and writing it on the back of our jackets with masking tape.
Adam Y

They were just the same as they are now, loud, obnoxious and ugly, and a lot of fun rather than a serious hardcore band. Whereas other bands, just as awful as The Beastie Boys, would actually believe they were good, for Mike and Adam the whole point was to be terrible – and to admit it.
Kate Schellenbach, the Beasties' original drummer, on the band in 1981

Nobody talks about my separate bands, we've all had separate bands since we were 14, my bands being the better separate bands. Tensions? Yes, an intense amount. It's a jealousy towards my apartment sort of thing.
Adam H, July 1989

In '80 or '81, we were going to shows. Everybody had bands back then: there was Even Worse, Awfuls, Stimulators, Bad Brains… More than half the kids who hung out had bands, so it seemed kinda natural to just start a band.
  We started one as a goof. That was kind of before punk turned into hardcore. We were just gonna put together a coupla songs and play a coupla shows.
Adam Y, July 1997

Our first gig was at A7, then we played at the Playroom opening up for Even Worse and HR was there. When we started playing, he started

moshing into everyone. So all the other kids started getting into it because they saw HR (Bad Brains' vocalist) was into it.

I went up to him afterwards and he was like, "Yeah, you should open up for us at (legendary New York punk club) Max's." So that's how we got on that show… That was our third or fourth show.
Adam Y, July 1997

When we first started in rap we played The Disco Fever (a club with a bad – as in mean – reputation) and The Encore in Queens. We played at the worst black clubs before we had any records out, that was really weird.
Mike D, October 1986

The Disco Fever? Yah. We were a bunch of faggots jumping around, we didn't know what we were doing, we tried to rap; we were f***in' idiots. They were lookin' at us like 'Who are these stupid f***in' white kids trying to rap?'
Adam Y, October 1986

We hooked up with Rick Rubin because we wanted to MC in our live shows and needed a DJ to do so, and he had turntables. He definitely swayed us in that he told us to forget the other stuff we were doing and just concentrate on the rap stuff.

He had this PA in the room and we'd listen to all the new 12-inch singles in there and Horovitz would make beats on his drum machine.
Mike D, July 1998

We needed a DJ and Rick was the only guy we knew with all the equipment – including, for some reason, a bubble machine which was straight out of *Saturday Night Fever*!
Mike D, 1994

Rick (Rubin, producer of *Licensed To III*) came into the picture after we did the record 'Cookie Puss'. That was sort of weird, it was right after Malcolm McLaren was making his records and

11

we were just having a good time. We'd been listening to hip-hop in rock clubs since day one, asking rock DJs to play the records, then we decided to do our own jam.
Mike D, 1986

After we did 'Cookie Puss' we were still a rock band, and we decided that we wanted to work some rap into our set, and this DJ said we ought to meet this guy Rick. It was Christmas, and we wanted to have a bubble machine and a smoke machine – Rick had both.

So there was a part of our show when Mike was playing the drums and Kate, who was our drummer, played the bass and Rick (DJ Double R) was scratching and me and Adam were trying to rap.
Adam Y, 1986

That show was at this weird sort of art place, a government-funded thing. We played clubs like the Danceteria and weird gallery places.
Mike D, 1986

Before that, we used to play hardcore clubs like CBGB's and Trudy Miller's. There was this bum who decided he was our manager for a while, Neil Cooper, and his mother owns an art gallery. He started making a lot of phone calls for us. We'd get like $500 for a show, which was way better than we'd get at CBGB's, we'd get like $100 there.

Rick started Def Jam Records when we were ready to put out 'Rock Hard'. We were talking to different labels, and we decided f*** it, we'll put it out on Def Jam.
Adam Y, 1986

Each of the things we started began as a little thing and then blew up into something bigger. The Beastie Boys itself started off as a dumb joke just to do a couple of gigs.

We always looked up to Dischord Records, and although we're not nearly as DIY as Dischord we were definitely inspired by them. Our own first record was put out by a friend of ours after he saw us at our first gig on my 17th birthday party.

Adam Y, November 1997
We recorded the first stuff on four-track. There was this record store that was in the basement of a studio. And the studio used to have benefit gigs, because inevitably they'd have to pay that month's rent… Bad Brains would play, people like that.

   I remember that, by the time we came to use the studio, they were losing their lease, and the heat had been turned off. It helped us get through our one takes even faster.
Mike D

When we did 'Cookie Puss' and 'Beastie Revolution', we were trying to cut a whole record. We recorded at a place we'd never recorded at before, and it was really kind of disastrous. The only salvageable moments were where we were just f***ing around, which were 'Cookie Puss' and 'Beastie Revolution'. I can't stand to listen to either of those things now, but that's just me.
Mike D

I don't know if we're the best band in America, but we're certainly having the best time.
Unidentified Beastie Boy, 1987

We definitely change when we're together, and I don't know why that should be. Maybe because we've known each other so long, who knows? It's inexplicable to me but all I can offer up is that I don't know why anyone would even want to talk seriously with us when we're like that.
Mike D, July 1998

I don't think we're particularly making dance music, we're more just writing, playing and recording the music we like and having a good time.
Mike D, May 1987

For all three of us, music is our whole lives. Since I was 13 and punk rock was the first music I listened to. It came along at the right age for me. Now I'm 23, I'm never going to like music the way I did between 1978 and 1980 because I was so blown away with what was happening.

A lot of record company employees don't even know what they've got on their own back catalogue. Trying to get record companies to do packaging that's different is like pulling teeth.
Mike D, July 1989

I'm starting to feel tired again, going through it all seems so strange. This is Yauch's analogy. It's like getting on this rollercoaster. You get on the ride because it looks like fun, you get on and you're pretty sure about it, you're going up the hill, and the car's going real slow, and now we're at the point where we're just about to peak.

Next week when we make the video will be the peak, and it's at the peak when you start regretting you ever got on the ride. Then it's too late and you just go down into the whole thing.
Mike D, July 1989

I think that we're more like cows that have been out to pasture returning to the feed barn. The band started as a joke, our intention was never anything more.

It was something like, "Okay, let's just have fun, this is a joke we'll do because it's funny." And as the band has evolved we've tried different things along those same lines. "Oh, let's try and rap, that'll be pretty funny." Then it'd be, "Let's attempt to pick up our instruments again," having no idea how those things managed to work. And what we're doing now is no different to what we've always done. So be it.
Mike D, January 1998

One possibility is that they would think "What's wrong with these guys? They

don't drink beer and they're not breaking stuff." It's kind of an impossible question to answer, though.

Would they have our records? I don't really know. But musically, there's still the three of us. There's still something that happens between the three of us – on stage and in the studio – that hasn't changed.
Mike D, September 1998, on what the 1987 Beastie Boys would think of their 1998 counterparts

How do I fit into the band's internal chemistry? Well, I like to work really fast. I spend most of my time ruminating on what I do, but when I get into the studio I get it down on tape really fast. The boys are actually very slow. They're very democratic, so an idea had to go around all of them several times before it's acted on...

They've always got a force behind them. Whether it's the Dust Brothers or Mario (Caldato Jr, producer since 1988) or me. That always seems to work for them. Their great strength is in collaboration. They're very resourceful that way. And they're just very good at what they do.
Keyboardist Money Mark, September 1998

I auditioned for (the movie) *Lost Angels* and the director didn't really know who I was. It wasn't like the producers said, "We gotta hire this kid because he's a rock star, girls are gonna come and see this film"... I just studied every night and practised and got the part. I wanted to do it so bad I got it.
Adam H, July 1989, on his brief film career

I think we're all pretty capable. At certain times I look to Yauch for leadership, and for that matter, even Horovitz at certain times. I think we're pretty unique in the way we work as a band, although it wasn't completely smooth getting to that point. If somebody has the vision or the sight or the initiative to make an idea happen, the other two will just be supportive, say "Okay, go with it." Then some ideas come from sheer combustion between us.
Mike D, March 1995

America Today
The Boys on their homeland

Not only did Columbus smell the gold and lie about landing (in the United States) first, he also looked like Elvis!
Adam H, June 1989

We have the most mixed group of fans of any tour out there. We get an equal share of black kids and white kids, which is what is so great about rap and rock merging.
Mike D

In a lot of the Southern states (of the US), just to own *Licensed To Ill* when your Dad's probably in the Klan is pretty subversive. And that's the sort of thing I'm glad we're responsible for.
Adam Y, December 1998

New York (in the 1980s) was a different city to how it is now. For a start you had a totally integrated club scene, which has never been the case anywhere in America and isn't the case in New York now. And it was wide open musically.
  Hardcore punk and rap was happening pretty much concurrently in the city, the punk clubs were the first to play rap records for a white audience and so as hardcore petered out, what was left? There were still incredible, ground-breaking rap records coming out. I remember at the Danceteria they'd play Kurtis Blow, then Spoonie G, then the Cure's 'Boys Don't Cry'. It was all, in this weird way, considered dance music.
Mike D, July 1998

Maybe it's because we were younger but (New York) seemed more carefree; cops were more lenient. I'd come back from school and everyone would be smoking pot on the train. There were all these theatres on 42nd

Street where you'd meet people and everyone would be smoking pot and angel dust in the actual theatres which definitely wouldn't happen now.
Mike D, July 1998

Actually, we were the first, er, 'honkies' to be on the cover of *Vibe*. We're pretty cool with *The Source* as well. But you can't really worry about it. I think it's kinda cool that we've been around long enough to get props from these kids coming up now who listened to our shit when they was, like, two. Or eight.
Adam H, March 1995

It's weird because I'd have to say, speaking for the three of us, I don't know how much we identify... I would definitely call myself Jewish, but I was brought up in basically a religiously ignorant setting. Purposely. Not that I'm saying that's right or wrong, but that's the way my parents were, straight up. We were almost, in my opinion, too devoid of any spirituality.
  When you're in Germany, in Austria, whatever, it can be a little weird. But in Britain also, because people don't ever make a big deal over this in the US, but they do over here.
Mike D on the 50th anniversary of the Holocaust, March 1995

To me, the subtext is... the British press make the biggest deal out of it. I don't know it that makes Britain a country that leans towards being anti-Semitic, or that across the board, being Jewish is the exception as opposed to the rule. Whereas, growing up in New York City, it was more a case of who isn't a Jew?
  I'm really glad it hasn't happened, but I keep waiting for it to happen, the

17

One of the (Buddhist) monks said something that's relevant here. He noticed this huge separation in America between the kids and the adults that doesn't exist where he comes from, and that there's a real polarisation between adults and youth.

nightmare of some skinheads showing up at the show but our audiences are cool. Knock on nylon tablecloth.
Mike D on the 50th anniversary of the Holocaust, March 1995

The weird thing now on tour, going to all these cities, is realising that white America, yeah, they really don't have the vaguest idea of what's going on. They don't know that there's a huge f***ing community in Los Angeles of kids who don't go north of Jefferson Boulevard, they're kept down below. They don't go out of a two-mile radius, that's how segregated it is.
Mike D, June 1992

I think a lot of people are seeing that the system doesn't work. I think they'd rather just go to work and pretend it's not happening, but what happened was a lot of people turned on the TV and simultaneously, round the world, thought, "Woah, what the f*** is going on? This isn't working." It's got to change. You've got a lot of people with no power, no money, no control over their lives. And that's got to be redistributed one way or another.
Adam Y, June 1992

Where they come from, when there's a celebration – or a dance, or a party, or music – the little kids and the grandpas are all dancing and singing together. That's something this country could definitely grasp hold of. Our polarisation of that is more extreme than it needs to be.
Adam Y, 1997

I think that New York is harder and more immediate, so you're constantly in contact with other people, like when you're walking around or on the trains. You're face-to-face with people all the time. It makes the music feel a lot harder and a lot of times the music we make in LA feels more introspective – more about being in our own little world

The people I come in contact with are just our friends, and the band. Whereas in New York, you're just walking down the street by millions of people, all day. On your way to the studio you're riding the train with people everywhere. So it has a different kind of feel, more of an outward feel.
Adam Y

The good thing about this album (*Ill Communication*) is we recorded part of it in New York and part of it in LA, so it's got both of those things going on.
Adam Y

Los Angeles enabled us to create our own world. We were able to build our studio… by having our own little world and studio we can create

whenever we want to create, at the pace we want to create, however we want to create. That's given us that feel – not just being in LA. It would've been very difficult to have that feeling in New York.
Mike D

I'm a little bit more of a transient than the average American. I have most of my stuff in storage right now. Then I'll move to Utah to snowboard in the winter, and then I'll put it all back in storage and go on tour in the summer. Los Angeles doesn't feel completely like home to me. I always feel a bit like I'm visiting, like I'm waiting to get some place else.
Adam Y

I feel no compunction to defend LA. People criticize it, and for the most part it's well-founded.
Mike D, May 1992, on his new home

Half the people in New York our age say they're in The Beastie Boys.
Adam H, May 1992

The US is this incredibly wealthy country that continues to disregard life of any variety, human and animal. And we're supposed to be the fortunate, developed ones.
Mike D, December 1998

When the US government started firing missiles to assert its authority and solve problems was one of those

moments which made me feel like apologising to the rest of the world...

I think that so many countries must look at us as this repressive nation who just resort to military might.
Mike D, December 1998

China being granted Most Favoured Nation trading status is an outrage. It once again exemplifies that our elected officials are working in the interest of big business and not working in the interest of humanity, not working in the interest of the American people.

Those people who choose to make an argument solely on a business level and ignore human rights – you know, that it's creating jobs or helping the American economy – they're wrong. It's actually creating more of a deficit in the American economy. It's taking away American jobs.
Adam Y

Boeing started doing business in China, then started a factory there and shut down an entire factory in America, where thousands of people were getting paid $30 an hour, or whatever they got paid, and now they're only paying a couple of dollars an hour. So now the trade that's actually going on is damaging the American economy directly.

The only people that are profiting from this are a select few upper-echelon people who run our corporations. Our government is run by big business, not by the people...
Adam Y

My hopes are, that in a year from now, when Most Favoured Nation status comes up, that everyone will be up in arms about this, that there will be demonstrations in campuses around the world, and that the people of America will no longer allow corporations to guide our government.
Adam Y

The strangest moment was when we were on tour over the summer when (President Bill) Clinton was going on air to make his 'non-apology apology' (for the Lewinsky affair). We all got on the bus, grabbed a beer, tuned in the TV, and it was like watching a football match. Apparently, it was the most-watched thing in America.

If as many people voted or became active as watched that, America would be a different place. People are way more interested in sexual scandal, I guess.
Mike D, December 1998

Fight For Your Right...
Goodbye Def Jam... Hello Grand Royal

It really boils down very simply. We got ripped off, and it sucks. It's a story that's been repeated over and over again. What's very sad about it and what's very embarrassing about it is that it's not like some unique, first-time situation. You read about it all through music history. It's a shame people still haven't learned from this.
Mike D, September 1989, on their $2 million royalty claim over _Licensed To Ill_, released on Def Jam

It's just not cool and makes you mad when you don't get paid for what you do. We're fortunate to be away from the whole Def Jam/Rush situation. It's real bad and we're extremely lucky.
Adam Y

Not getting paid was the tip of an iceberg that went much deeper. We toured for longer than we wanted, we were put through a lotta things we didn't wanna do, that we weren't really into.
Mike D

We hung out there (the Mondrian Hotel, Los Angeles) last year, that was def. We used to hang out on the roof and that's where Russell's guys tried to slap the subpoena on us. For two days they waited outside our rooms because you just have to be touched with the subpoena and you're caught, it's like a game. We got security to chuck them out…
 We called all our friends up in LA and got them to come over with disguises and we were all dressed up and Yauch had a big curly afro wig and I had long robes and they were trying to get at us but couldn't work out who was who.
Adam H, July 1989

The Def Jam logo? Huh! What does it stand for now – Defunct Junk?
Mike D, July 1989

We're not really interested in talking about what happened, it sucks. When we made the deal with Def Jam we made the mistake of it not being just based on business but based on a friendship that we thought we had.
 We couldn't have made this LP _(Paul's Boutique)_ with Def Jam. We couldn't have done the covers. I kinda respect the fact that Rick (Rubin) left. He wanted to get away from everything and we wanted to get away from everything, I suppose.
Mike D, July 1989

It's kinda hard to be friends when someone's given you so much shit, when someone's treated you so

badly, you can't. I'd like to just go up there and talk to Rick about The James Gang or something, there's shit he doesn't even know about, I'd sit there and play him The James Gang and he'd play me some shit I'd never heard.

made us learn, all of a sudden we had to do a crash course in record companies and in six months we just about learned everything. And what pissed me off is that record companies don't seem to listen.
Mike D, July 1989

I don't miss that though because that's what I do with (Dust Brother) Matt (Dyke) now. Sometimes it feels like we all moved on and (manager) Russell (Simmons) was left holding the bag and the blame, but at the same time Rick is to blame as well. It was such as extreme situation I don't know how you can ever work out where to place the blame.
Mike D, July 1989

The thing about all these manipulator guys like Russell and Malcolm McLaren is they take what essentially happened by accident and they take the credit for it. Who do you talk to during the hiatus? After that how can you trust anybody? You've got to take some time.
Switching record companies really

Part of the myth bands get stuck into is that they can't do business on their own behalf because they're purely artistic. It's something that works in favour of the record companies more than anybody. By perpetuating that myth, most bands are convinced that they couldn't possibly deal with the business – but in reality, if they focused just a little on it, they could deal with it as well (as), if not better than the people they have around them doing it.
Mike, July 1997

I'd like to say I have no animosity towards (Def Jam boss) Russell Simmons. But that would be a lie. How can you not dislike someone who stole from you?
Mike D, June 1989

Leaving Def Jam was kind of a blessing in disguise, because now we can make whatever record we want.
Mike D, May 1992

I heard Russell (Simmons) was getting mad at us because we

As soon as (Luscious Jackson's *In Search Of Manny*) came out I realised that I didn't have the first clue of what the f*** I was doing. Getting the press was easy because it was the first thing we put out and we thought that would be that. We didn't realise you

didn't want to throw beer at each other any more. And that was our job.
Adam H, May 1992

Columbia Records looked at us as the curse of the whole (Def Jam distribution) deal.
Mike D, 1996

We used to sit around for hours coming up with these ideas. But we never did anything about it. Jill (Cunniff, Luscious Jackson singer/bassist) kept asking if we knew anyone who might put their demo out and suddenly we thought, "Why don't we do it?" The fact that we stopped talking about it and actually did something was miraculous…

had to physically phone up each and every store and ask them to stock the record. Now we employ two people just to do that all day.
Mike D, July 1997, on the birth of the Beasties' *Grand Royal* label

I guess I do do most of the label stuff, although at times both the Adams are involved. I'm helping to get the label going and growing while Yauch is more on the philanthropic side of things. He'll help some of the bands that he has a special relationship with, give them advice and whatnot. Adam Horovitz, well, he is consumed by music. All day long he is making beats and playing with guitars, drum machines. And yet we do have our

main day jobs. Although we're busy, we haven't lost sight of that.
Mike D, November 1997

Everything we put out is so radically different. We're not a label focused on one specific sound. I wish I could sign bands purely based on their love of food, but most of them aren't interested in eating at all. But there's no big plan. Most times I sign a band it's through fortunate proximity more than anything. They'll just happen to give me a tape, nothing else.
Mike D, July 1997

I figure the whole point is to take risks, but I guess that's contrary to how people practise good business. That's what makes me different from the rest. The only reason I want success is to be able to have the money to do other projects.

You have to realise that what a record label does is really pretty absurd. You're putting out music by people and you're actually trying to make it popular. That's a completely absurd act if you look at it from an outside perspective. It's fun to figure out how to do it, but it's definitely a ridiculous concept.
Mike D, July 1997

This is going to sound really corny, but for me the basic rule is just do things that make you happiest and ultimately hope that that will work out. By being basically very naïve I think we've managed to remain pretty true to that.

That's why my ambition for the label is very simple. I just want to get to the point where the things we are putting out are successful and we can continue to put out whatever we want. I'd like to repeat what we're doing now in the UK around the world, just have small offices in different countries filled with people who we trust and who can put forward our music honestly.
Mike D, November 1997

Grand Royal's kind of like hair. You can do with it what you want. When we started we had no idea. You do need to be successful, though, if only to continue to put cool records out.
Mike D, January 1998

Without wishing to sound too boring, we just figure that as opposed to having our records come through lots of little labels, we'd like to have the situation we enjoy over here in the States where we have our own autonomous world. That way we're not dependent on someone else understanding what we're doing.

Most labels are a little more concise in terms of the scope of what they put out. We're radically all over the place. Everything we put out is radically different to the last thing. You know, currently we boast the recording services of the likes of Ben Lee, Butter 08, Buffalo Daughter, the Josephine Wiggs Experience and so forth. We're not a label that's focused on one sound. We're rocking to a whole bunch of styles. I think that's to our benefit.

I hope it's to our benefit, anyway.
Mike D, November 1997, on the idea behind a Grand Royal UK office

What we're looking for is an energetic, dynamic personality, combined with business acumen, artistic passion, Zen meditative qualities and overall crowd appeal. The ability to move a crowd is a vital consideration, although these are all important criteria for this person to have. I would also like them to be able to juggle in the bath. Otherwise, need not apply.
Mike D, November 1997, on The Beastie Boys' search for a Grand Royal UK representative

This is just insane. This trip is so hectic. I'm really tired and spaced out. But it's got to be done. In America all our projects have turned from a barge into an ocean liner, and now we're floating that liner over here…

It took us a while to reach an illusory state of competence in the US. We've given ourselves the illusion that we know some of what we're doing, so we're now ready to go beyond that. Now is the time. I consulted a lot of clairvoyants and Tarot-card readers and had people perform different ceremonies and that's what all the signs pointed towards.
Mike D, January 1998, on the UK launch of Grand Royal

I used to go down this dock area in Los Angeles, where all the shipping companies and merchant marines are based. All the dock workers used to get these really cool work clothes from stores around there. I'd never seen them anywhere else, so we planned to do our own store on a really small scale, just selling this kind of stuff. Then at least we'd have a place to get the stuff that we wanted to wear without having to go so far.
Mike D, April 1995, on the Boys' clothing marque

Beyond people thinking we had nothing to do with music and never asking us questions about music, people would come up to us and say, "Heeey! That's great all you guys, who told you to wear those hats and sneakers, the whole look is so… I want that for the next project I'm working on."
Adam Y

It's all about taking a fashion risk. Go into a store and look for something which you really don't know if you can get away with. But if you can pull it off, you have scored a fashion victory. On the other hand, you can look like you always dress that way 'cos it's what your mom buys you. Like you just… don't know any better.
Mike D, March 1995, on fashion

We started with the store on Vermont, here in LA. As with everything else, the idea came first and the practicalities second. The idea was that we wanted to sell clothes we wanted to wear. We'd have to travel down to the docks to get this workwear we liked, so we thought, 'Let's make this stuff available nearby.'
   T-shirts (were the first to be produced), because they're the easiest to make. Then we started to do knock-offs of the stuff we liked to wear, the workwear, but in cotton instead of polyester. It's the same learning curve as the label or the magazine: you quickly find out that quality is the most important thing when stuff falls apart or shrinks to half size after washing.
Mike D, July 1997

The magazine was another mistake. It started because people were writing in looking for the lyrics to *Check Your Head* and it was costing us a load of money sending those out, so we thought we could start a magazine to communicate with fans… and then we lost even more money.
Mike D, November 1997

We didn't sit down and think, "Hey, let's make a magazine." It was more pathetic than that. We had all these people writing to us about the band and we weren't getting back. We had this simple ambition of a newsletter, but then we saw a couple of other bands' fanzines and they were just like, 'This is what the band's up to now and this is what they'll be doing.' We were like, 'No way! So we made it into a proper magazine… And then somehow we got delusional and out of control and way too big.
Mike D, July 1997

What's up with *Grand Royal* magazine? We got Mark Lumen, former editor of *Dirt* magazine aboard. Actually, dude, shit has really been coming together this week in the magazine. Because this whole thing… you know how we're doing something on Dick Hyman, right? And we're doing something on Weird Al and it turns out that Dick Hyman has played on some of Weird Al's records!
   Anyway, so Russell is gonna be in LA in the end of November so we're gonna set up an interview and everything. It like, all ties together. Well, we have bigger plans than that but I don't want to divulge those…
Mike D, 1994

This is an extremely collectable magazine. All the time I hear about people going to other people's houses and sitting there, sitting in the toilet reading it. It's phenomenal! Its coffee-table life, its shelf-life is just huge.
Mike D, July 1997

I love learning things and being challenged by new problems. Also, the fact that the goals aren't primarily financially motivated, that takes away that desperation and leaves the fun part. It's fortunate that it's not my major source of income…

Sometimes (business-speak) scares me. I'll catch myself speaking like that, but with some people you almost have to use a different language, a certain mode of operation. But it scares me, the prospect of getting totally immersed in the business side.
Mike D, 1997

There's still rewards I get from the band that nothing else compares to. Playing a show there's a lot of gratification you don't get anywhere else, but having that first issue of the magazine in my hand was the same as having our first record in my hand. We were working in the studio when the magazine came in. We sat around all night, unable to believe we made this… thing.
Mike D, July 1997

The Beastie Boys are really open people, and Grand Royal is a really open label. The whole premise of my initial relationship with them was like, "Why don't you release a 7-inch of that weird tape you recorded on your beatbox?" I played some tapes for Adam (Yauch), and he'd been to the shows I did with my mom. He wanted to release that, without my name on it. His whole idea was to be really alternative about it.

Just the opportunity to release anything on Grand Royal was like, "Wow!", 'cos they're so cool. It slowly evolved into going into the studio, but Grand Royal were prepared for something way more out there. That's why they're so great.
Sean Lennon, September 1998

They were certainly an influence, like, "Wouldn't it be cool to do something like the Grand Royal or X-Large approach?" It's nothing to do with success – they do things if they're a good idea. They know they've got people who'll buy anything they're associated with and they use that to push things that are off the beaten track. I'll always admire that.
Skint label boss Damien Harris, September 1998

Men Behaving Badly
Beer, babes and the bad boy image

We're thinking towards a good time, we're thinking towards the consumption of beer, towards a person who's more interested in pussy than keeping a nine-to-five job, we're talking about a hedonistic attitude to life…
Beastie Boys 'manifesto', 1986

We're just normal guys. We like to have a good time, play a little music: we don't base our entire reality on fashion.
Adam Y, 1986

I'd like to say hi to all the Puerto Rican ladies listening out there.
Adam Y, June 1989

This woman called up my mother this week. Her daughter dropped out of high school because of us; it made me feel really bad.
Mike D, 1986

A lot of the time, if you're drunk and you're having a good time and someone throws a lamp against the wall, and you're laughing and someone wants to outdo him, so they kick in the television, and then an ashtray goes through the window. And pretty soon you're laughing that you're actually doing all these clichéd things and having a good time.
Mike D, May 1987

We still haven't quite crossed the border into where all the cool people totally hate you.
Adam Y, 1986

Our lyrics? Girls… drinking… girls… drinking… getting drunk with girls… getting drunk without girls… hanging out with girls without being drunk… basically, fairly sexist drunk records.
Adam Y, 1986

When we're talking about women or whatever, we're creating a fantasy. What we're doing is creating a fantasy, so far-fetched and overboard that the 99 per cent of the people that understand it understand that there is such a thing as humour, such a thing as parody.
Adam Y, January 1987

Do any of our lyrics upset people? The only people who beef about it are the people who are supposed to beef about it. Like the girls' fathers!
Adam Y, 1986

Basically what we are saying is that The Beastie Boys like f***ing women with big floppy tits and nipples like omelettes.
Adam Y, 1985

This is the gay area and I've lived here all my life and I hate faggots. I really do… I shouldn't have said that. I've got a lot of gay friends but… you don't know what it's like growing up in this neighbourhood.
Adam H, 1986

The reason Adam hates gay people is that in this neighbourhood, when you're five years old, when you're walking down the street a lot of 'disgusting' faggots who hang around here aren't like just gay people – normal gay people – all the sickos who are gay hang about on Christopher Street and they see kids and they walk up to them and they say 'Hey kid, I'll give you five bucks if you suck my dick', y'know.
Adam Y, January 1987

Most people who seem intelligent to me, they get the joke and they think it's funny… but when I meet people who are really *stooopid*, they either agree with the lyric or they fail to see the humour. Look, I can honestly say that nobody, nobody, has ever come up to me and said – "Hey! Girls to do the dishes, that's an excellent idea!"
Adam Y, January 1987, on the band's over-the-top lyrics

A lot of the humour wasn't interpreted in a way that we might perhaps have envisaged.
Mike D, September 1998

Taking all those people, different sorts of people, and putting them all in the one concert hall, they're gonna see what we do on stage – laughing and spraying beer on each other. They have a choice, they can either have a good time, really go with it, or they can say "Man, they're really f***ed up" – and leave.
Mike D, January 1987

I have seen Run DMC in their dressing room like throwing bottles of

34

ketchup against the wall and breaking chairs and shit and no-one ever writes about it. A lot of other bands probably do shit a lot worse than us but we get the press because we're a bunch of little white kids.
Adam Y, January 1987

Sometimes we have f***ed shit up, destroyed parties, and blown up hotel rooms. But it's not anything we feel we need to do. The main thing we enjoy doing is making music. I'm not that bothered by it all, I'd rather read in the press about our music than all that.
Mike D, May 1987

I want these diabolical creatures banned from these shores.
Conservative MP Geoffrey Dickens, May 1987

At first we were The Monkees, then The Sex Pistols, then Frankie Goes To Hollywood…
Mike D, July 1989

We were just making music that we liked, stuff that was funny to us, and then all of a sudden it became this big, controversial thing. It's almost sort of like we don't feel responsible for it, because to a large extent we're not.
Mike D, September 1989

What most adults don't understand about most teenagers is that most teenagers are extremely conservative most of the time, even as they are engaging in obnoxious behaviour designed to differentiate themselves from most adults.
  Most teenagers enjoy a heavily structured life, are threatened by deviations from the conforming norm and will ridicule those enamoured of deviating from the conforming norm. In this way, most teenagers are exactly like most adults, the only difference being that teenagers piss their lives away in high school while adults piss their lives away in corporations. Most teenagers do, after all, grow up to be most adults.
  Adam Y, 1987

I guess managers... take responsibility for what is basically a bunch of people doing the right thing in the right place. But you can't keep on doing that or else it isn't genuine. The very thing that made you be like that suddenly becomes boring and predictable. It all comes back to the age-old issue of "It's easier to hit a man on the back of the head with a vodka bottle when he's not expecting it than hitting him with it when he's looking."
Mike D

Ah man, Liverpool. Three songs in and we realise that all the audience are singing, but not one of our songs. So we asked our English friend, the Captain, what was going on and he said, "It's really bad, they're singing football songs." Then the bottles and cans started flying in from everywhere.
Adam H, 1998, on the Beasties' infamous gig at Liverpool's Royal Court Theatre in 1987

Miraculously I don't think I got hit – and we were like ducks in a shooting gallery! After about three songs it was obvious that it wasn't going to let up, so we just had to down tools and get out of there. Once we were on the bus we thought, "Thank God it's over. All English people are assholes."
Mike D, June 1996

The police turned up at the Portobello Hotel in London where we were staying to arrest Horovitz on a charge of having assaulted a girl at the Liverpool gig. She claimed she'd been hit by one of the cans he'd batted into the audience. They carted him off and it was quickly decided that Yauch and I would have to get out of the country before they came after us too.
  We had four or five days to kill before we flew off to Japan for dates. My girlfriend and I went to Italy and had a great trip, actually. We weren't being disloyal to Adam, but there was nothing we could do for him.
  Mike D, June 1996

I spent the weekend in the police cells, which was a drag because it was a long weekend. I never threw a thing, I was totally innocent. I had this big-shot lawyer who hated me because not only was I American and rich, I was American, rich, young and jewish.

But I was innocent; even the girl and their one witness said they hadn't seen me do it. By the end of the trial the lawyer even quite liked me. Then we left court, shook hands, opened a paper and there was a picture of me giving the double finger. His face just collapsed. Asshole.
Adam H, July 1998

Nobody could have planned it to build up to that (in Liverpool). We went on stage and before we even got on there were just hundreds of bottles going everywhere. We got out of there and there's just this mass of hate and riot. A mass of people hating and fighting and throwing and drunk and f***ed up. What did we have to do with that apart from just being there?
Mike D, July 1989

At least I wasn't alone. My friends were all there sharing it with me, in a way. Do I recognise myself? Think of the time you were the most drunk, hugging the toilet, f***ed-up and ugly… but in a happy way. Do you recognise that? Me, too. We toured for nine months in '87, made fools of ourselves, but we had fun and people were into it.
Adam H, July 1998

There were all these headlines – Brawling Beasties, Beastie Boys Go Bonkers, Pop Stars Flee Night Of Terror With Beastie Boys, Beasties Back On Rampage – and Russell was telling me to go and do more interviews with them to try and sort it out. And I was going, 'You don't understand, they're making this shit up.'
Adam Y, July 1989

My job with the Beasties was to try and cause as much chaos as possible on the road and build the press story as we went along. It didn't take long for Britain to go to town on the band.
John Reid, Beastie Boys' road manager, June 1996

If you saw where we came from and then looked at the rest of America, I don't think you'd think what we're doing is an endorsement of the American way of life, because what we're doing is so different. When you get out to Davenport, Iowa, or Nebraska or wherever, and we do our show, it means a whole new different thing to them than it ever did to us.
Mike D, May 1987

It's like when we had the dick (a hydraulic penis that formed part of the Beasties' stage show at one point) and everything, it seemed real funny because we were told we could have whatever we liked built for the stage show. And then in Davenport or England or wherever, it turns into a whole new different thing.

Like it almost killed me when I heard that this MP was making a fuss and that they all stopped the Parliament and the next point on the agenda was they were going to decide whether we were going to be allowed to come into England and play. That made me feel great.
Mike D, May 1987

There were debates in Parliament about whether we should be allowed to perform in Britain and whether we should be allowed to bring over our 'inflatable' penis, which was actually hydraulic. I've always had this visual image of very earnest people in wigs discussing the merits of a hydraulic penis.
Mike D, June 1996

Britain was just farcical. I remember standing on stage at the Brixton Academy with the police and fire people from Lambeth Council assuring them that on no account would there be any 25-foot penises on the stage while leaning on a box containing… a 25-foot penis!
John Reid, June 1996

We'd paid two girls to dance in the cage and they sold their stories to the *News Of The World*, but there were still queues of girls at every gig wearing leotards and trying to get to dance.
John Reid, June 1996

We vowed that we'd never go back to England after that tour – we hated the place – but when we finally relented and came over with the *Check Your Head* album nobody gave a f***. It was poetic justice really.
Mike D, June 1996

The whole press thing blew up when we performed with Smokey Robinson, Sting and a load of others at this TV special in Montreux during the early part of our European tour with Run DMC. *The Mirror* ran a story about the boys laughing at crippled kids who were at the show and that upset everyone because it wasn't true. We did deals with a lot of the journalists who were out there to keep the press thing moving, but that was out of line.
John Reid, June 1996

This *Daily Mirror* journalist, Gill Pringle, had been hanging in Montreux trying to get a story and she had asked Adam Horovitz for a few words. He blew her off because he didn't have time and because she'd been snubbed she just made up the entire story.
Mike D, June 1996

I remember getting off the bus for a show in Offenbach and everyone was talking about this news story in the *Mirror* that accused the band of beating up cripples. We were all

astounded. The band kept saying "Why are they writing this shit?" There was a lot of resentment. From then on there were 20 or 30 tabloid 'animals' in pursuit all the time.
Agent Paul Boswell, June 1996

When I read it I was really pissed off. I felt powerless to convince anyone that it wasn't true. We didn't sue the paper although we did consider it. It would have been too costly. There was actually a small retraction printed much later but by then the damage had been done. I had to phone my mom and tell her I wasn't really a cannibalistic, child-eating mass-murderer.
Mike D, June 1996

American group The Beastie Boys deny all allegations in the *Daily Mirror* that they jeered at or made derogatory remarks to children at the Montreux Rock Festival. The trio, after a hectic day of interviews and press conferences, met with a group of children from the Dreams Come True organisation, signed

autographs for them and were delighted to be able to spend time with them. They were shocked and upset by the reports in the *Daily Mirror*. Legal action is being considered by the band.
Official Def Jam statement, May 1987

I didn't see one kid in a wheelchair the entire time we were in Switzerland. We were in the middle of a radio interview and this woman came in and said, "Will you sign this autograph book?" I said something like, "Not now, we're in the middle of an interview." She said, "It's for a crippled kid," so we stopped the interview and passed it round the band.
  We have two friends who are both paralysed from the neck down, one from cancer and the other from a motorcycle accident, so I don't think that we'd be making jokes about cripples. A child who has to be in a wheelchair for the rest of their life is not funny.
Adam H, May 1987

I don't know if you can print what I think of those papers. They're just pathetic rags. I know what I've done and what I haven't done. The whole thing just means that we don't want to come to England any more which is a shame because the kids are really into us and we like them.
Adam H, May 1987

We tried to keep the parental advisory sticker off (*Paul's Boutique*). It's really weak, it was really wack. It's even wackier to me when people take new songs like 'High Plains Drifter' or 'Looking Down The Barrel Of A Gun'

and talk about The Beastie Boys' violent tendencies. They don't understand. That's a character narrative. Why is that any different than (William Burroughs' novel) *Naked Lunch*? If that came out in this day and age it would probably have an explicit sticker on it.
Mike D, September 1989

The time when, erm, Dan Aykroyd and Jim Carrey came by and we did coke for four or five days, that was pretty cool. We had a whole bar set up, too.
Adam H, September 1998

So anyway, I'm sitting in Taco Bell, minding my own business, eating a bean and cheese burrito with my homeboys, when 5-0 steps in. At least thirty young Mormon faces turn and stare at us as the officers approached, asking for ID.

After querying. us about some supposed graffiti piece on a wall not far from there, which I denied knowing anything about (as any good fool would do), he asked to see my hands – which, coincidentally, had the same colour of spray paint on them as the mural in question. Officer Attitude immediately claimed that he had witnesses who had seen me do the piece and questioned my integrity in front of everybody…
Adam Y

On a more serious note, I thought it was a public wall, owned by the city. I wouldn't have done it if I knew it was private property. So I offered to pay for them to repaint their wall and they dropped the charges. What was the mural of? 241, Mikey's clothing company.
Adam Y

Of course it gets boring being asked to call someone a dick, that's just stupid unless you really think they are. I don't think people made us do things but by the end you'd walk into a room and people would look at you and expect you to 'throw that can of beer' or 'tell them to f*** off' or whatever it is we were 'meant' to do.
Adam Y

After *Licensed To Ill*, I was living in LA, really introverted because of too many drugs. Then coming into *Check Your Head* I stopped doing all that. I was already wishing for some way to be able to be a benefit the world.
Adam Y, January 1998

I don't drink as much as I did before. I think I drank too much for a while.
Adam H, July 1989

Am I still taking drugs? No. I don't even drink or smoke or anything. It started out as something that worked for me, and I've got more regimented about it recently because it's nice to have a policy. I'll go to a party and see some friends and they'll be like, "Come on, have a beer." It's just easier to have a set decision that I don't drink than trying to decide if I'll have one beer, or maybe I'll have two beers and wake up in the morning with a headache.
Adam Y, 1997

I stopped smoking herb three or four years ago. The one thing about doing hallucinogens is that they open up your solar plexus chakra and allow you to take in the energy of every body else around you, whether you want to or not. Hallucinogens blow that chakra wide open and you can start taking on a lot of negative energy – worries, jealousy, anger, or whatever other contractive emotions are flying around. I just can't even mess with that now. I feel a little more in control by keeping my energy separate.
Adam Y, 1997

At this point, who I am and what we do is accepted in the fashion world. But in a lot of ways, in straight-up, high-fashion circles, I feel pretty awkward. I still feel like some badly dressed bum who they shouldn't have let in off the street…
It's like, if I go to a place where there's, like, eight supermodels hanging around, I can't help but feel like I belong back on the subway riding to high school, because I look like some kind of spliffy bum.
Mike D, April 1995

I feel grown up. I like the grey because it makes me look like a maths teacher or a movie star.
Adam H, September 1998, on his prematurely greying hair

During the course of putting together *Grand Royal* magazine, the issue came up several times of whether or not to censor or change certain things. On the one hand, I didn't want to deny anyone their freedom of speech, but on the other hand, I am very aware that we are drawing the attention the band has to other people's opinions, which in some cases I don't agree with.

The things I feel the strongest about are (articles) which glamorise the idea of having and carrying guns. I definitely understand this feeling. Until recently I used to try to present myself that way too. After growing up on Clint Eastwood movies and bad TV, who wouldn't think it was cool?
Adam Y

(Non) Musicians Only
The Beastie philosophy of music-making

Black kids are always hipper to what's going on than white kids. What's so good about rap music is that it's always changing. You'll have new records on the radio all the time, while on rock stations they're still playing 'Stairway To Heaven'.

Black stations like KISS and BLS have these rap hours on Friday and Saturday and it's all new stuff. The rock stations have, like, 'The New Music Hour' and they play Madonna and the Stones album and y'know, it's like 'new music' that you're going to hear every day for months.
Mike D, January 1987

White people are terrified to go to a rap show, they're terrified to go to an all-black show. White people are definitely scared to cross over to the other side of the tracks. Maybe we're making it all right now, maybe we're making it safe.
Adam Y, January 1987

We didn't know if we were ever going to be able to play to white people ever… I mean we had the feeling that we'd maybe only be able to play to black people, I mean that's still our number one audience. We started off playing to a black audience.
Mike D, January 1987

What makes us significant is we're a white rap group, and we're performing for this audience that's never seen people like us.
Mike D, 1987

I always wanted a bass when I was a kid, though I didn't get one at first. My parents were too tired of buying me things that would just end up in the closet. I knew this girl who had a bass, and I'd go over to her house to play. My parents eventually rented one for me on the condition that if I played it, I could have it.
Adam Y

For my 12th birthday my mom and all her friends got me a guitar and a little practice amp. I talked about playing guitar all the time – so my mom and her friends bought me a Hondo II Professional.
Adam H

When our first hip-hop records came out ('Rock Hard' etc), there weren't really any other white kids out rhyming. It's possible that there might have been other white kids who rhymed at block parties or whatever, but if so, it was a rare occurrence and they weren't making records. So, when we started making hip-hop records, it hit first in the black community before it did at all with the white kids. Most white kids outside of New York had never heard of hip-hop.
Adam Y, 1996

At the time, a lot of people, having just heard the music, thought we were black. When people finally met us and saw that we were white, they were surprised, not that we sounded black, but just because it was out of left field to have somebody rhyming who was white. It wasn't until later when *Licensed To Ill* came out and 'Fight For Your Right To Party' that it started to flip to a white audience.

At the time, a lot of hip-hop lyrics spoke about unity between the races. There was little or no racial tension in hip-hop.
Adam Y, 1996

I've got nothing against Adrock, but he writes a lot of the lyrics that we can't use 'cos they're just sick in the mind.
Mike D, 1986

I write about a weird guy… walking down the street… with beer! He (Mike D) writes a lot about standing on the corner drinking beer and going to the deli and getting food, that's right up his alley.
Adam H, 1986

Darryl Jenifer (Bad Brains bassist) is the musician who most influenced my playing. Though the stuff I play now is in a different vein, if you listen to our hardcore tracks, I think you can hear his influence. I've seen them like 50 times. I climb up on something where I can get a good view of Jenifer's hands. He's an unbelievable bassist.
Adam Y

Attitude-wise, hardcore and rap are remarkably similar. The energy is the same. And you can express yourself without having to study music for 15 years. I used to say the only difference was that with punk rock you have funny haircuts, whereas with rap you have funny hats.
Mike D, 1992

We got tired of the hardcore scene. It was very negative. The rap scene is a lot better because the rappers all have more camaraderie with each other.
Mike D, 1987

If you're not going to have as much equipment as AC/DC, you really shouldn't play instruments. When we can be as rich as them and have that kind of stage show, we'll play instruments.
Mike D, 1996

I'm happier with the music now than I've ever been, even when I was on guitar.
Adam H, July 1989

We've been listening to everything from Bad Brains to Eddie Harris, Lee Perry, Funkadelic, The Stooges, Buddy Rich, Ornette Coleman, Spoonie G, The Headhunters, Cypress Hill. The good thing about the sampler is you can create the best

possible collaborations. You can have Yauch, Ron Carter, Hendrix and The Meters all jamming at once.
Mike D, April 1992

I started listening to reggae when my brother moved out and I was able to

develop my own tastes. It was probably *The Harder They Come* soundtrack that turned me on to it. I got these (singles) from the hottest record shop in San Francisco. Old soul singles from the mid-Seventies. I never know what's on them but there's always some classics in there.
Adam H, April 1992

So what's up with Adam and Adam? Smoking crack! No, I don't know. We've just been doing our thing. Have you been keeping it real? I would say, yeah, keeping it real. We got the bicycle crew in effect…
What about Adam, it's his birthday today, right? How old is he, 28? No, I think he's 29 now. The same age as me. What did you get him? We got him that guitar a little while ago – me, Adam and Mario. We all went in on that. That jazz-type guitar? Yeah, that dope Gretsch hollow-body. That's cool – he must have been psyched. He won't be able to smash that one though. No. That one's a nice one. He can't break that one.
Mike D, 1994

A lot of times, when I'm focused on the Tibet stuff and Mike's working on the label, this guy (Adrock) is going nuts on the SP1200 (sampler). A lot of the beats on this record are all stuff that Adam's made over the last couple of years on the SP1200. He's got just boxes and boxes of disks.

Adam Y, 1998

I have this plastic mechanical box called a sampler, that's the SP1200 thing. It's like this, and the record player's there, and then you put the record on and it records into the thing. Then you can sort of chop off a little bit in front and a little bit at the end so you get exactly the part that you want. I become completely obsessed with it. It's like playing Tetris or video games. It goes over and over in your head when you sleep.

Adam H, 1998

When we first started recording, everything was played live. We have a drum machine, so that they play to a click and we can go back and sample or whatever. But generally, the first month or so whenever we jam, we just press the DAT. Occasionally, somebody'll have a sample of something we like and we'll loop it up and they'll play along with it, just to get a vibe or some kind of feel…

Basically, we have a turntable set up there and when we're not jamming, we're listening to records. Occasionally Adrock will programme some cool beats on the Akai SP1200 and we'll listen to those and they'll maybe play along. The SP1200 is the hip-hop machine basically and it's simple and quick for him. He's pretty much mastered it. But the general focus is mainly to play live as much as we can.

Mario Caldato, *Hello Nasty* co-producer, August 1998

I have to push them a little and say, 'Let's start doing some rap joints.' They always hesitate on the rap stuff, because they don't like doing the lyrics and stuff. I guess they're just really conscious of what they say at times. Then once we do one good song, they'll start rapping.

The Dungeon is their rehearsal place and it's got an eight-track and mixer that we bought and I helped them set up. They started jamming and doing songs on their own. They ended up doing a record of 12 country songs because they were actually thinking about doing a movie, some comedy or something. But the idea started off small and turned out to be a big Hollywood studio thing, so they decided to pull the plug before it became too ridiculous.

Mario Caldato, August 1998

We used the panty hose – and I mean that with all due respect – technique on the microphones (for *Hello Nasty*). On our last couple of albums we used these special mics that were built for us that had a certain distorted sound, but this time we went back to a high quality Sennheiser, a German microphone, with the panty hose in front of it to avoid any pops, any unwanted things of that nature.

We spent a lot of time hanging out at each other's apartments, working on rhymes together and splitting 'em up, instead of each coming in with our own thing.

Mike D, on the songwriting for *Hello Nasty*

Adam was talking to this guy about the song 'The Payback' by James Brown. And the guy was trying to say that the guitar was playing nothing. But see, I figure, well, if the guitar is playing nothing, then that means the entire band is playing nothing. But, then, that's the best playing ever on, like, any song. And they're all playing nothing.

That's the best shit. To be able to do that, that's the funk. Unfortunately, people confuse the funk with a lot more superfluous musical activity.
Mike D

There's no way we'd ever think we could compete with the jazz session guys. I look up to Bernie Purdie, but I can't compete with him. The goal is just to play grooves.
Mike D

The whole thing with being a fan of music and buying records is that you're constantly coming across grooves of records that are gonna change your life. That's the cool thing about music, I'm never going to run out of discovering those records and those records are never going to stop coming out.
   There's always going to be some group that comes out that changes everything, or there's going to be some group or some group of records that I discover that I didn't know about before that's going to be everything for me also. So it's two-fold, it's like that's going to change my life and it's going to change what I do.
Mike D

I would say that if this album (*Paul's Boutique*) is saying anything, it's saying that we love music. That is, indeed, the central statement in my eyes.
Adam Y

I think technology just works its way into what we do. We might buy an old piece of equipment, but it's new to us and by fooling around with it we produce a certain kind of sound that ends up on a record.
Mike D, July 1998

Most musicians I grew up playing music with would probably shoot me if I ever complained about selling 800,000 records. It's definitely not a number to sneeze at.
Adam Y, 1992

When you sample the type of music we do, you come to respect the incredible musicianship that went into the original. And you want to be able to play like that.
Mike D

We have pretty short attention spans. When we're working on our own we end up with so many different ideas that we're not confined to just bass, drums, guitar for any given songs. Trying to narrow it down to the ones that work the best is the trickiest.
Mike D, July 1998

Cuts like 'And Me', 'Instant Death' and 'I Don't Know' were more emotionally raw and we thought they sounded honest, so we didn't mess with them too much.
Mike D, July 1998

It's funny to me that there are all these people who listen to our records and knock us, yet probably don't know any of the history we do. All we do is sit around and listen to records and music all the time. It's weird for me to think that there are people who sit around and don't listen to records all the time.
Mike D

We were going for that Latin-1960s-mod-psychedelic TV show vibe. We had a demo of a song that Adam had made at his house, which definitely did not have that vibe. So we came up with the concept of adding the sitar guitar and trying to make it like a mod-psychedelic trip.
   Of course, when we ended up actually making it, it was slightly different to what we actually said we were going to make. But that's the process of music.
Mike D, July 1998

People come to interview us about everything but the music, which is weird because if it wasn't for the music we wouldn't be there and they certainly wouldn't be there…
Mike D, July 1998

The In Sound From Way Out
The Tracks That Made Their Name

'Polly Wog Stew' (12" EP)
The first record really came out of going to see bands like Bad Brains. But in terms of us growing up and listening to music, the shows where we first met up come from an earlier wave of music. We'd go and see people like the Slits, Gang of Four, Delta 5 and the Raincoats. We were borderline new-wavers!
Mike D

The first band we had was kind of like our fake-Slits band. The first band you have is always the one where you say, 'I'm gonna try and play music like that' – and you try to emulate the music you've been listening to, completely miss the point and end up doing something completely different.
   Then, when hardcore came in, we thought, 'Yeah, we can do that, and wouldn't it be the funniest thing in the world if we actually played some shows!' So it happened. And at the same time hip-hop came to our attention.
Mike D

'Egg Raid On Mojo'
Mojo was this huge guy we all knew who was kind of like a nightclub chameleon. You'd see him out at a club and he'd be ska, then the next week he'd be new romantic, and the week after that he'd be punk rock.
   Then he started working on the door at nightclubs and being a real dick, not wanting to let us in because we were underage. So we had to take matters into our own hands, and bring out the heavy artillery...
Mike D

'Cookie Puss' (Single)
'Cookie Puss' was the name of this ice-cream cake that you get from a chain of stores in America. Whenever you came in from a club, you'd turn on the TV and there'd be these late-night commercials for it.
Mike D

We were trying to do an album and we made 'Cookie Puss' by mistake. We just got

bored in the studio and we weren't liking anything that was happening so we just said, 'Let's record a disco thing. It'll be really funny.'
Adam Y, October 1986

We were getting a black audience... but we couldn't play 'Cookie Puss' live; the only thing we could do like it was rapping.
Mike D, 1987

'Rock Hard' (Single)
At the time we were psyched and making 'Rock Hard' was very exciting, although pretty embarrassing to look back on.
Mike D, July 1998

'She's On It' (Single)
The guitar on 'She's On It' is kind of wimpy by comparison to 'Rock Hard'. The 'Rock Hard' one was really hard heavy metal with us screaming these raps. A lot of people liked it, more people who were into heavy metal didn't. But it's true we don't know that many people who like heavy metal...
Adam Y, 1986

B-boys liked it 'cos it was, like, really loud. The fact that there was guitar in it didn't matter as long as it was loud. I kept saying 'Speed up the tempo, Speed up the tempo!'
Mike D, 1986

Yeah, we were up to 185 beats per minute and Mike's ass just started dancing.
Adam Y, 1986

Licensed To III (Album)
We want to call the album *Don't Be A Faggot*, but somehow I don't think they're going to let us... they won't accept that as a working title. It has nothing to do with being homosexual, it just means being a wimp and not standing up for what you believe in. It'll definitely be a cut on the album at least.
Adam Y, 1986

This album is going to have a real tilt towards telling people they have very boring everyday lives, and to stop being suckers.
Mike D, 1986

It's a parody of music today and full of inside jokes.
Adam H, 1989

There are some things that I think are really fly and still stand up and there are songs that I am completely embarrassed to be involved with.
Mike D, 1996

I was only 21 when *Licensed To III* came out and that record was just the sound of the three of us goofing off. Everything we did was stupid. When we were asked what kind of stage show we wanted the first thing we could think of was a giant dick, so we had one made! It seemed the obvious thing to do at the time.
We used the dick down in Alabama and Carolina and completely freaked everyone out. We were immediately banned and they passed a Beastie Boy Ordnance outlawing outrageous and immoral behaviour in a public place. That was where the British tabloids first picked up on us.
Mike D, June 1996

You've just got to look at (*Licensed*) as a piece of fiction. Like a movie. Same way you see a bunch of people shooting each other, burning down villages and shooting heroin. It's not real – it's just some ill shit. Parts of it were pretty radically exaggerated, there's definitely things about smoking dust and raping and pillage – which is shit we do all the time now – but at the time we hadn't started doing it. You know what I'm saying?
Adam Y

What boggles my mind is that (*Licensed To III*) remains one of the biggest-selling catalogue records. We never envisaged the longevity and neither did Russell (Simmons, Rick Rubin's partner). He was used to rap records being big for maybe a couple of months. It still sells something like 500,000 a year. Too weird. I just wonder if it's people wearing out their old copies, or if it's 14-year-old kids just getting into it now. Either way, it's still too weird.
Mike D, July 1998

'(You Gotta) Fight For Your Right To Party' (Single)

The only thing that upsets me is that we might have reinforced certain values of some people in our audience when our own values were actually totally different. There were tons of guys singing along to 'Fight For Your Right To Party' who were oblivious to the fact it was a total goof on them. Irony is oft missed.
Mike D

Paul's Boutique (Album)

Yauch's legs were broken from skiing, my yacht had capsized and Adam had a bad back from playing too much croquet, so we really didn't have much choice, but really I think the silence has helped us in the long run. We are talking about The Hiatus here. The Hiatus is over.
Mike D, 1989

It wasn't until we actually got together to make *Paul's Boutique* that we realised that the three of us were The Beastie Boys, it was weird. It's taken two years but I'm kinda surprised that no titles have been taken. Music's still the same, uptight all the time.
Adam H, July 1989

Will *Paul's Boutique* change the public's mind about us? Not until we have a boxed set are people's minds really going to change.
Mike D, September 1989

There's a discrepancy because some people want records to come out and we really don't do records like other bands, we don't follow those schedules that other people do. You can't just sit down and do it, it took us nearly two years to write the first album.
Mike D, July 1989

It's a nice feeling (working without Def Jam). I don't think they would have let us work with three unknown guys who had only done a few indie records. It was very different and more fun. It was kind of cool working with normal people.
Mike D, June 1989

I think it just ended up being dense. It's almost adult-oriented rock, but of a kind that doesn't exist. Everything throughout the album meant something – it's not like there are 20 minutes of filler. It will be interesting to see what happens.
Mike D, June 1989

Russell did say that if we came out with *Paul's Boutique* again and wore our baseball caps sideways we'd sell eight million records. Says people are ready for that shit now.
Mike D, May 1992

On *Paul's Boutique* there's a song where I am starting to say what I'm feeling spiritually. It's called 'A Year And A Day', but the lyrics to that song aren't on the lyric sheet and I'm using a real distorted mic, so it's not really clear. And I got a lot of positive feedback from people. I was kind of taking a big risk for myself doing that, just in terms of my own confidence, but I got a lot of positivity on that.
   Then there were a lot of positive lyrics on *Check Your Head*. That kind of thing goes back and forth: when I hear that people are into it, it makes me feel more confident.
Adam Y

Before this album, Matt Dyke (one third of the Dust Brothers) flew us down to his club, Powertools, and we've been friends ever since. Then when we came out here to LA to work with him it was strange to hear the reactions… "Matt who?"
   Now people look at it and say, "Oh, last time Rubin, this time Dyke's the big name in rap." Which is of course uninformed and stupid, but what can

you do? Let me tell you, here is a man who had sold millions of records, doesn't have a dime and lives in a bummy, stinky apartment. He hasn't been paid yet either!
Mike D

I used to know Matt because he ran clubs and then I met him again when they were launching Delicious Vinyl in New York. It reminded me of the first Def Jam party in London when LL's first LP and our single were just out. It kinda had the same vibe to it, like it was going to take off in the same way. Then Tone Loc's record became this huge seller.
Mike D, July 1989

Check Your Head (Album)
People who are making hip-hop records definitely understand where we're coming from, because they're used to hearing funky instrumental shit. People who only listen to hip-hop in hip-hop form, it might be a little hard for them to hear at first.
Mike D, May 1992

A lot of the theory this time was okay, let's make a record that's like all the dope break parts of the records we listen to. We wanted to play because we were inspired by the music we were listening to all the time.
Mike D, May 1992

The bottom line with a lot of bands that funk is being applied to is that they don't really listen to funk and aren't versed in funk. Like, you know, Gordon Lightfoot.
Mike D, May 1992

People think it's taken so long to do this album, but it kind of seems like when we were doing it it only took a few months.
Adam H, May 1992

We could have released this stuff as six different phases on six different albums. Isn't that the trend now? Instead, it's just six different phases on one album.
Mike D, May 1992

We wanted to make (*Check Your Head*) like a breakbeats record. The same way as when you sample you take the best bit of a song, we wanted each song to contain the best bits from our jam sessions.
Mike D

Every song came out differently. Lots of times we had songs done in rehearsal, and we'd go into the studio and try to improve it. But after we restructured it, we would end up going back to the original. The feeling was the thing, not laying down some perfect performance.
Adam H

I've definitely played along with my fair share of Meters records, and I love War. It's not hard for me – I've been doing that ever since I was little. I guess when I was like 13 and got my first set of headphones and was really listening to different instruments, I got really into bass. I was listening to a lot of Bob Marley back then, bugging out on 'Family Man'.
Adam Y

We just messed around a lot. We kept playing around with the music and stuff, slowly putting things into place until they were done. We'd actually planned – hoped – on finishing a lot sooner. We kept making deadlines for ourselves and kept missing 'em. It goes back to school – we were definitely constantly absent and late back with our term papers and asking for extensions.
Adam Y

We rocked a distorted mic effect that has confused a lot of people. There's some people who realise how fly it is, but there's some people that just

aren't with it. Some people think it was by accident, but really, they don't understand that we tried a bunch of different microphones until we could find mics that sounded like that.
Mike D

I'm getting freaked out now that the album is starting to sell a little bit. I'm trying to learn how to be comfortable with that. I would never deny anyone the pleasure of selling a lot of records, but it's strange for us. We're this group that's just totally passionate about music and just playing around, and all of a sudden everybody's into us.
Mike D

'Some Old Bullshit' (Compilation of first two EPs)
A lot of kids would write to us asking where they could get hold of this stuff. And all you could do was either buy the original pressings at really inflated prices, because they'd become collectors' items, or import CDs which were also a total rip-off. We've got our own label, so it just seemed to make sense to make it all available again.
 I didn't even have the original demos. I just had a cassette which I recorded off the radio, from this college radio specialist show, so you've got all the radio compression on there. That's one way that this stuff links up with what we're doing now. Our goal is always to make people think that their stereos are broken.
Mike D

Ill Communication (Album)
In a lot of ways we did a lot of stuff with *Ill Communication* we wouldn't have been capable of doing before. At the same time, with *Check Your Head*, there was a lot that we learned about making a record that we applied to *Ill Communication*. This album was a lot about applying everything that we had learned on those records to this record.
Mike D

I have taken the Bodhisattva Vow, but I would like to clarify something. A lot of people have the misconception that taking the Bodhisattva Vow delays enlightenment until all other sentient beings attain enlightenment, and that is not really it. The Bodhisattva Vow means striving for enlightenment to better help all other sentient beings attain enlightenment. That's an important issue – the objective of that vow.
Adam Y, 1997

Being enlightened is the best way to benefit all other beings – from that point you are able to help more. The Dalai Lama helped me clarify that – because I was hesitant about taking the Vow. He said something that clarified that point and I said, "Ah, all right, cool."

Did I have an audience with him? No, that was incorrectly reported in the press. I happened to catch him when he was walking out of a room. It was wild. He grabbed both of my hands and looked at me for a second and I felt all this energy. I just walked to my room and it clicked in my head. I thought, I need to write a song about this.
Adam Y, 1997

Aglio E Olio (Mini Album)
The hardcore EP is going to come out down there (Australia). But I think we might also put 'Light My Fire' on it or something. We got this girl Miho from the group Cibo Matto on our album and she's all that and the group Cibo Matto is all that. We're like a cross between Jose Feliciano and like, the Young Hope Version. Ours is more smoothed out… on the Japanese hardcore trip.

Right now it's called 'Aglio E Olio'… you know, like when you go to the restaurant and you order Spaghetti Aglio E Olio and it's like, with garlic and oil. It's just spaghetti! It's like, the most common dish in Italy! It's just

spaghetti with garlic and olive oil. Low budget! You could make that meal for yourself at home for probably like, a whopping 98 cents! But just to let the kids know, it's eight songs but only ten minutes. It's important to let the people know…
Mike D, 1994

Unreleased Material
We have too much material that isn't good enough to be on the record and not enough stuff that is good. When we get enough good songs we'll stick it out.
Mike D, November 1997

I have two CDs' worth of our new songs right here and we are working hard to turn these into one CD of stuff because not even Wu-Tang Clan can put out two CDs of stuff. Within those two CDs, anything could happen. All I can say is that we are definitely dropping some styles we've never dropped before. But at the same time, we're going to rhyme school and on that end we are doing some stuff that perhaps only we uniquely can do.
Mike D, November 1997

Hello Nasty (Album)
The album's at a sort of middleness stage. It's the stage where we're starting to get a little more serious than the last stage. We're down from three albums' worth to one and a half.
Mike, January 1998

We started off doing stuff we haven't done since *Paul's Boutique*. Like, we were hanging out at each other's apartments working on lyrics together for the first time in years, so our voices just drop in and out a lot and we sing each other's rhymes. The last two albums we'd turn up with our parts pretty much written, but this was more fun.
  I think we try and get a balance when we write. There's something

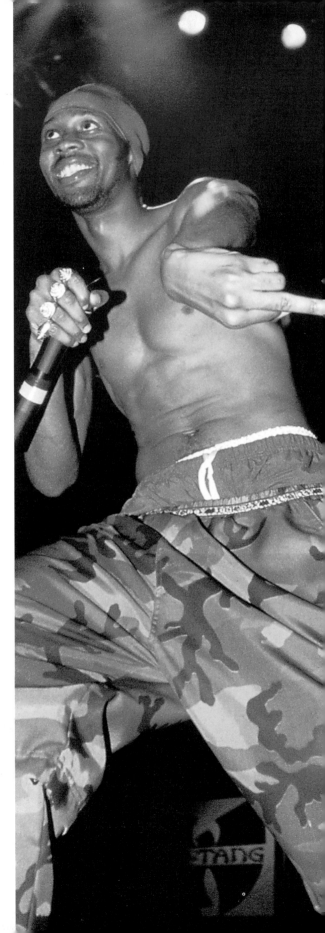

that happens when we get together and start writing rhymes. We go for integrating the goofing around that comes with us three being in the same room, and the serious intent. I hope.
Mike D

They basically play their standard instruments – Mike D on drums, Yauch on bass, Adam Horovitz on guitar, (Money) Mark on keyboards – but on this record, there's actually a lot of changing around going on.

Adrock played drums a lot. Occasionally, y'know, somebody else would play guitar or get on the keyboards. But that was the main change on this record, that Adrock got behind the drums for a couple of songs. He was actually the most involved in the songwriting of the record, far more than the other guys. I'd say, like, 75 per cent of the record is his responsibility.
Co-producer Mario Caldato, August 1998

We had (Money) Mark come out, and basically before he got there, they only played hardcore. When he came out, we hired a Hammond B3, and in like, one week or something like that, we just did about 20 songs.

When they're jamming, I'm basically in the control room, messing around. If it sounds good, I'll roll the multis. If they're just mucking around, then I'm just rocking the DAT and just trying a bunch of effects to see what compliments the music. Then they'll come back and listen to the tapes and go, like, "Aw yeah, that's cool, let's try this and try that." Basically, it's a lot of jamming and a lot of reviewing and picking and selecting what we like.
Mario Caldato, August 1998

Why the title? I don't know. It started with this Japanese friend who was working at the place that does our

publicity, Nasty Little Man. She used to answer the phone, "Hello, Nasty!"
Mike D, July 1998

Ultimately we set out to plagiarise the funky breakbeats but weren't able to. So it became totally our own sound through sheer incompetence.
Mike D, December 1998

For the whole first half of this record our attitude was more, 'Let's get together and play music'.
Mike D, July 1998

'Intergalactic' (Single)
When I knew that they'd heard of Skint, I was like, 'Oooh, my God…' Just to get the opportunity to do a mix (of 'Intergalactic') for them was great. Unfortunately we were in the middle of moving, so it ended up being a rushed job and the version we sent them didn't blow anyone away. But I was honoured to be asked because they're so influential. There's just something

about their humour and their rhymes that really gets me excited.
Skint label boss Damien Harris, September 1998

We were in the space station working on the record, in orbit of the planet, not this planet but the planet which we were in orbit of, working on the record, and a robot flew up through space to the space station singing the chorus for that particular song ('Intergalactic') and beckoned us to climb into his papoose and fly to Earth. Which we did without hesitation.
  We landed in Japan and sang this song together, which was documented and is going to be the video. Then we climbed back into the papoose and returned to the space station to continue work on the album. So, in a sense, the robot chose the single.
Adam Y, July 1998

Some of the stuff you hear on the album is really just us playing in this room, or stuff we did years earlier and others playing live. Other stuff is really

where we've just chopped up little bits of stuff that we all played together where maybe we were playing on the tape for maybe 15 or 20 minutes and we just took three seconds. But that can be the primo three seconds.
Mike D, 1998

Puffy (Sean 'Puff Daddy' Combs) is one of the songwriters we're talking to, but there are a number of songwriters we're talking to. There's a number in the country arena. Whoever is making hits.
Adam Y, 1998

I don't want to give away particulars about the outfits or specific routines, but for those who are watching, if you're familiar with *Fame* or *Flashdance*, these kinds of things are going to be worked in… a lot of exuberant dance numbers.
Mike D, on the Hello Nasty Tour live show, 1998

We didn't have the idea for the video really worked out before we left. But somehow it all miraculously came

together and became all about Japan…
 Everyone told us beforehand that we absolutely must not film (on the Tokyo underground) without permission, that you have to write to people weeks in advance and it's a nightmare. So we basically broke every rule.
Mike D, December 1998

There was only one time where it went wrong. We were in this downtown area and started filming in what turned out to be this really important government building. When we started filming, these security guys came out and started yelling at us, so we ran. Then it turned into something out of the Keystone Cops, more cops joined the chase, and when we got out onto the street, some more cops cut us off.
 There were a couple of times where we'd suddenly start playing the song and we just went for it. There were people sitting there and you could see them thinking, "Oh no, what now?"
Mike D, December 1998

Beasts On The Road
Globe Trotting With The Masters Of The Mic

*It was nuts. We'd open for Run DMC in a club in Queens or wherever and everyone had heard our records, but then we'd turn up, three white kids in Puma shirts, and (Madonna's) audience would be, like, "What the f*** ?" But they were usually into it.
Mike D, July 1998

We opened for Kurtis Blow and UTFO at this hardcore black disco club called the Encore Club. We had to talk our way inside, the club was so full. The place smelled like a cross between mentholated cigarettes and angel dust. We go on and people looked at us like we were out of our minds. We were honestly, genuinely alien, in the truest sense.
Mike D, 1994

I remember one night doing a gig in a real rough part of town with Kurtis Blow and it was touch and go whether we were going to get out alive. We (got) stared at like we were from outer space, which was a little disconcerting. In that kind of situation, you have to be good at what you do or you're dead.
Adam H, 1994

Landing the support slot on Madonna's American tour was real cool. We just went to every city and made eight year olds' parents upset! It was like the cool thing to hate us, just because everybody hates the opening band.
  I think a lot of people liked us because everyone else was booing, and when they thought about it they liked us. Girls would come back and be like, "Oh, those guys don't know what they're talking about, I'm so embarrassed. I really thought you guys were great."
Adam Y, 1986

Well, Madonna, we did go on tour with her and it was Russell Simmons' greatest coup. At the time she was just becoming massive and wanted to retain some cool, so they rang up for Run DMC – but they were already pulling in $80,000 a night and they couldn't afford to pay that so Russell told her that he had this other band, the White Run DMC, who'd do it for half the price and that's how it occurred… and it is true she took a shining to Yauch.
Adam H, April 1992

They were going to throw us off the tour after the first few nights, but then our manager went and pleaded with Madonna in her dressing room and she decided not to kick us off.
Adam Y

They came on stage in front of 20,000 screaming 15-year-old Madonna wannabes, saying things like "Don't you love us?" The booing was deafening, so MCA jumped on top of one of the speakers, grabbed his crotch and started insulting the audience in very graphic language. I expected lightning to come down and strike him dead.
Publicist Bill Adler, December 1998

Licensed To III Tour
I think of that tour every time we come to the UK. There were times when things got a little out of hand, but there were funny times, too. English journalism is so extreme – it's a real love-hate thing. Lately the press has been really positive, so I'm wondering when we're going to turn the next corner and get barraged in the other direction.
Adam Y, January 1998

What do you think about what happened? You go on tour in England and everybody says horrible things about you, you play in a riot, and then you go on tour for four more months than you really want to. It's beyond drudgery, it gets to the point where it's worse than the guy who sits on the bridge in the toll booth, you're doing that for months.
Mike D, July 1989

The first time we ever went to London, we went to this place called Alice In Wonderland and there wasn't any place like that in New York that you could go to. People consider heavy metal or rock in the States as that pussy Bon Jovi shit, Guns N'Roses bullshit. But that place was cool because it didn't play anything from the Eighties. You know what was really def was that German disco they played all the time at the Mudd Club. That was really wack.
Adam H, July 1989

The time that I felt battered was in Europe. We were getting battered. Wake up in the morning, read the paper, and be battered. It just got depressing after a while because it got so far away from the intentions of why we do this. I wonder, "Do we really want to work so hard?" If there were people we could trust in the world then we wouldn't have to work so hard.

After making this record we got together and said, "Why go through with the rest of it? Why not just go back and make another record?" That's the fun part of it, you wake up in the morning, and you go to the studio and do whatever the f*** you want.
Mike D, July 1989

We're trying to keep it from being like work. I hope that eight months from now it's still good and we remain friends. There wasn't tension between us like three people in a room not

talking. It was three people in different rooms on three different phones to New York. Whereas before it had always been three guys in a room drinking the mini-bar. We just got sick of each other, which anyone would after nine months of touring.
Mike D, July 1989

Me, Yauch and Mike said, "Let's take a break and go and live on a farm somewhere and be friends rather than these f***ing enemies on the road", because our managers kept forcing us out there. For three months, touring was so much fun, and then it was four months, and a headache every morning.
Adam H, July 1989

We're going to tour here in the fall and then do a Christmas EP with some live stuff, and some unreleased, and maybe a track with Biz Markie. They want us to come to England but how do we know the same audience as

Liverpool won't show up? There're too many hazards at the minute.
Mike D, July 1989

We're going out in August 1989, and the tour will be short and sweet.
Adam H, June 1989

Since people are really terrified of going to rap shows now, we're going to bill it as a reunion tour because this is a reunion for us – and these ones are the ones that are doing big business. You know, the Rolling Stones, The Who, the Ringo Starr tour… Even though The Beastie Boys never broke up, we're going to bill it as a reunion thing and hop on that whole bandwagon.
Mike D, September 1989

When we're on tour we have a rider of four cases of beer, half a gallon of Stoli, Bacardi, and Jack Daniels for the rock'n'roll image but I don't think anyone ever drank it.
Adam H, July 1989

People are saying we should have Soul II Soul on tour with us but I don't know. We want a rap act and a band that we like, but I can't think of any. We had thought about Blue Cheer but how could we have gone above them on the bill? Maybe we could have Madonna and Warren Beattie in the cage, and Sandra Bernhard on the decks.
Mike D, July 1989

It was nice recapping old times to do those songs. But by the time we did the next show I was like, "Damn this shit is old." It was like bringing out the antique-coin collection.
Adam Y, May 1992, on the series of 1991 shows in New York which revisited *Licensed To III* material because they hadn't yet bothered to learn the *Paul's Boutique* songs

How does it feel to be coming out to Australia? I'm really looking forward to it because the vegetarian food is fine and so is the surf. And there's a lot more space too. The Summersault tour (of Australia) will be like a vacation with a lot of people that we know. That was the original idea of the concept or whatever. We might not be good friends when we start, but by time we finish it, we're going to be bosom buddies – all of us!
   This is not about money – it's just about hanging out and having a good time and playing with some bands that would be fun to play with.
Mike D, 1994

After Summersault, we're going to do Asia. I don't know, we're going to do Indonesia next year actually because there's this whole bullshit that went down with corporate sponsorship and we weren't really cool with that. I don't know, they were saying to play there we'd have to have the big cigarette company

sponsor the whole shit and we said we're not having it! I don't know what's going on with that. I shouldn't say for sure because who knows what the f*** will happen.
Mike D, 1994

We just thought that if we were gonna be involved (in Lollapalooza) this year, we should make it something that was more to our liking than something we just gave in to.
   We wanted to get away from playing at a rock festival, which was the whole idea of bringing in Tribe, Funkadelic and the Breeders, whom I definitely don't consider to be a rock band 'cos what they do is cool and so different. Let's just say we would have been a lot less interested in playing with Alice In Chains.
Mike D, September 1994

In Lollapalooza… everyone had their different cliques, right? And nobody would let Billy Corgan in any of their cliques! No, but in the real, Lollapalooza was a big commercial thing… all these bands playing together but it wasn't so much because they wanted to be playing together. It was more just like opportunity and money and all that type of shit.
   But you know, I don't even want to go into Lollapalooza. You had the juice clique, the drinking clique, you had the drug clique… Which one were we down with? Man, I was down with the f***ing enema clique!
Mike D, 1994

My big fear is jocks; that's my big fear for Lollapalooza. If I look out and see a big jock guy in front with a shirt on and his big, ugly sunglasses, I can't help thinking that this is the guy that our song 'Tough Guy' is about. Do you think he read our page in the Lollapalooza magazine? Probably not.
Mike D, September 1994

When we were doing warm-up dates for this tour, I would get really upset depending on how the audience was behaving. It got to the point where I just wanted to put my hand through the wall; I'd go back to the hotel really depressed and wouldn't even want to play anymore.

My thinking was that if playing music makes people behave in this belligerent and primitive way, there's just no point in going through this totally out-dated ritual.
Mike D, September 1994

To me, the indicative thing about how out of control the crowd gets is that we can be playing the most mellow instrumental and you'll see some kid floating on top and then going over. I understand that the music is high-energy and loud and if we're doing a hardcore song kids are gonna behave in a certain way, but sometimes it's really obvious that they're just not getting it.
Mike D, September 1994

I truly believe that kids are simply behaving in a certain way because they've seen it on MTV. When I was going to see Minor Threat or Bad Brains when I was 15 years old, yeah, sure, I'd be at the front moshing or stage-diving or whatever, but it was a very small scene. It was something that genuinely happened, whereas now you've got kids slam-dancing in Aerosmith videos. So kids are like: "Okay, that's what I'm supposed to do. I shouldn't be go-go dancing or having a good time in my own space, I should be doing that."
Mike D, September 1994

So we're going to Manila, Bangkok, Hong Kong, Tokyo… And we're gonna catch some ape gear over there. Let me think of what else is up… It's gonna be the whole band? Yeah, actually, for a while we were gonna do a strip down but now I guess (Money) Mark is gonna come down with us. Yeah, he's doing his own thing. It should be cool.

We have a whole new all male gospel chorus not unlike the Tabernacle choir. They sing on a couple of numbers, so that's nice. Well it's going to be hot. So we're thinking of coming out in leopard print g-strings. Yeah, I'm wearing a leopard print g-string right now!
Mike D, 1994, on plans for touring Asia after the Summersault tour of Australia

What we got into in Japan was like one of us would make a set list and not tell anybody else or show it to anybody else before we'd go on stage, so that way it would be like a jolt of surprise. To me that's always what rap is based on, just constant evolution and constant innovation.
Mike D

Japan is brilliant for vinyl. There's all this rare stuff that I've been looking two years for, and you walk into a store and you find it straight away. But it costs 200 bucks, so there's this thing where you think, "Do you buy it?" 'Cos if you do every time you play it you're just gonna be thinking of the 200 bucks. You buy it every time.
Mike D

Sometimes New York can be more stressful just 'cos unlike every other city you play in the world all our friends and family are here. Everybody we grew up with. It kinda compounds it by however many times.

It was a very intimate evening compared to what we have been doing of late. We've been doing sports arenas, 20,000 people. But in a way that show's been cool, we've actually been doing that with a round stage and it actually makes it a lot more intimate. If that's possible.
Mike D, December 1998

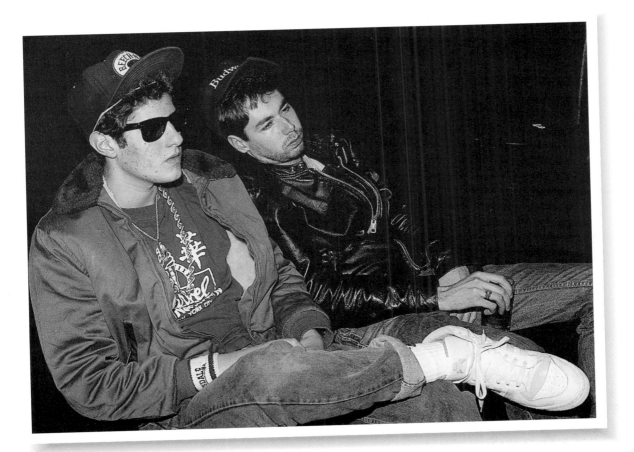

The show in Ireland was definitely a high point for us. It seemed that we'd landed in the middle of nowhere, and the landing was pretty scary. The weather was really bad, so we greeted that little airport with open arms.

It wasn't the performance we did that sticks in the memory so much, but that we played in the middle of this cow field and there were actually people there to see us. To us, it seemed like a minor miracle. When we got off the plane, we thought there would just be some cows and a few cow herders at the gig.
Mike D, December 1998

My daily practice incorporates all kinds of things that I've learned. I meditate in the morning and before I go to sleep. These are usually the main times, because before I go to sleep I can get focused on what happened during the day, pull that into perspective, and that'll make my sleep a little more peaceful. Then I set up what's going on the next day or get centred for those activities in the morning. A lot of times on tour I don't get a chance to because it's so crazy running around.
Adam Y, 1997

We've been all over your Europe. Last night we went to somewhere called, I dunno, Glllllllgmmmmfff. Reading is better.
Adam H, September 1998

I got a guitar and a little practice amp for my 12th birthday. I was listening to a lot of Kiss, and I wanted to be Ace (Frehley, Kiss guitarist). I thought 'Shock Me' – the song where Ace sings – was the shit! 'Making Love' too.
Adam H

Heros, Dopes And Bright New Hopes

From Kiss To Bis, The Beasties Pay Tribute

Punk came to America later than England. When we were going out to punk clubs in 1979, there were maybe 20 kids in New York into punk. There was Public Image, the Undertones and the Clash, and they were coming over but they had to become famous enough to be able to come and play America. And we were the first people listening to that stuff.
Adam Y, May 1987

We came across Johnny Thunders selling autographed 10" x 8" glossies outside Rat Cage to feed his heroin habit. Stiv (Bators), Johnny and most of the other Dolls are dead by now which, I think, underlines the redundancy of the era.
Adam H, 1994

Paul Weller's def, man. What happened to him? This is what I do all day. I play records and rock out in front of the mirror. You should see me when I put the Dylan songs on. I turn the lights out.
Adam H, July 1989

The first hip-hop I ever heard – really before it was ever on wax – was on the subway when I was going to school hearing kids playing battle tapes. As soon as (Sugarhill Gang's) 'Rapper's Delight' or 'Flash To The Beat' by Grandmaster Flash came out, we'd start to request them downtown.

A DJ who was influential – and this wasn't a hip-hop thing – was this woman Anita Sarko who used to play clubs like (the) Mudd Club. We'd convince her to play stuff. She played No Wave stuff, but also New Wave dance stuff. She was the first downtown DJ we could convince to play 'Birthday Party Rap' or 'Spoonin' Rap'.
Mike D, 1994

Another influential DJ was (Afrika) Bambaataa and that definitely changed the world for us when we heard him spin. First of all, he had this presence – not as a performer or someone onstage – but when he came into the place, him and his whole Zulu Nation crew, it was his presence. He just took over the vibe, dominated the vibe, he made the vibe.

The thing that really f***ed us up was that we expected him to play hip-hop jams, and he did, but the whole shit was mixing in 'Apache' or 'Son Of Scorpio' and then he'd go into the craziest pop record and make it work, like 'Oh Mikki, you're so fine!' That's what I mean by freakin' it. Bam could mix the most unlikely records and make it work.
Mike D, 1994

I went to see U2's film *Rattle & Hum* and afterwards I just thought, "How can you not be horrified with yourselves? How can you actually let this thing be released when it makes every single person in it look like the biggest asshole ever?" The whole statement is like, "We are mega stars!"
Mike D, June 1992

I'd just like to see Bono and Morrissey fight each other.
Mike D, June 1992

The Dust Brothers (Matt Dike, John King and Mike Simpson) played us a tape of what they had done, and that's what we wanted our stuff (on *Paul's Boutique*) to sound like. You could maybe use the word stew or pot luck or casserole, those type of terms. What you're talking about is combining a lot of different things, a lot of different seasonings.
Mike D, September 1989

The fact is that funky is the most misused word in music today.
Mike D, May 1992

A lot of people are getting over playing 'chink chink chink' on the guitar and people saying they're funky.
Adam H, May 1992

You just got to put on a James Brown record if you want to know what funky means. James was defining the word on a regular basis.
Adam Y, May 1992

Anthrax covered one of our songs for the Beavis and Butt-head album and that makes me feel very old.
Mike D, April 1994

It's only every so often a band puts out a record completely by themselves, like *The Secret Vampire Soundtrack*, and it becomes a hit without huge record company help. I thought that was cool. The way companies spend millions of dollars on figuring out how to get big sellers and then you get a band that makes a record in their bedroom and get an immediate hit… It's not as if I came over, contract in hand. But I ended up signing (Bis) anyway. Besides, they write better pop songs than I ever could.
Mike D, July 1997, on his interest in indie hopefuls Bis

Beasties vs Prodigy at the 1998 Reading Festival

We felt uncomfortable with the meaning of the lyrics of Prodigy's 'Smack My Bitch Up' and felt that if they were going to play the song, then we would be obligated to comment on it from the stage.
Adam Y, September 1998

When we called, we asked them if they would consider not playing the song. We explained that although this may sound hypocritical, we recently have been trying to be more careful in choosing what songs we play, as well as changing some of the lyrics in songs we do play.

They responded by telling us that the meaning of 'Smack My Bitch Up' was not what it appeared to be. They felt that they were in effect, subverting the meaning of the title. We felt that the meaning of the song comes across clearly and that it promotes violence towards women.
Adam Y, September 1998

Though it may seem strange coming from us, there seems to be a real abundance of violence towards women imagery in film, music, media, etc. And we felt obligated to try to affect change (by protesting to the Prodigy about 'Smack My Bitch Up').
Ideally it would have been in a non-

publicised manner. However, if the publicity generated promotes awareness and discussion on the topic, perhaps that is a good thing after all.
Adam Y, September 1998

We were trying to let (the Prodigy) know that there's things we've said on record in the past where we were maybe joking around and that those lyrics weren't actually taken that way. And that we were in the process of trying for ourselves to turn that around, or when we play those songs live actually changing some of the lyrics.
Mike D, December 1998

I think it all worked out fine, though. I mean, I don't know, 'cos we weren't in England and didn't see the press, but I got the impression it wasn't made that big a deal of.
Adam Y, December 1998

Where I'm coming from, 'Smack My Bitch Up' isn't very cool.
Adam H, December 1998

... a friend of mine... called me up right after the publicity came out about that dispute between (the Beasties and The Prodigy), and said "I'm really glad you said something because I was in an abusive relationship and my boyfriend used to beat me up all the time, and every time I hear that song I cringe, so I'm really glad you said something."
   So, clearly, to her those lyrics had a definite meaning. To us they had a definite meaning. And I'm sure that irrespective of each other, those

words have that same meaning to a lot of people.
Adam Y, December 1998

You know, a woman gets murdered in America every 20 minutes, every day, in domestic violence. Every 20 minutes. So 'Smack My Bitch Up' isn't that funny. I don't think. You know what I'm saying? And it may sound hypocritical of us to say that but OK, there you go.
Adam H, December 1998

I still respect their music, but I think they should respect other people's freedom to express themselves. As far as I'm concerned, the Beasties have got completely the wrong idea about what 'Smack My Bitch Up' means.
Prodigy's Liam Howlett, September 1998

Bentley Rhythm Ace! Yeah, I love that band. When we played live in New York I used, like, two bars of this one song of theirs for something we rapped over. What was that track? It's kinda like a hip-hop tempo and then it goes into this fast jump beat. It's called something like 'Bentley's Gonna F*** You Up' or some shit.
Mike D, January 1998

(Lee 'Scratch' Perry) arrived with the lyrics he wanted to sing written on the back of a poster for his show. It was Halloween and he was wearing his usual clothes – y'know, covered in CDs and notes he's written. There was a huge fancy dress parade down in Greenwich Village – he walked through it and nobody gave him a second glance.
Mike D, September 1998, on Perry's contribution to the *Hello Nasty* album

A weird thing happened recently, when me and my friend Spike were listening to the heavy metal station in LA. We imagined it was gonna be all

Sabbath, Zeppelin, Metallica, all the straight-up metal, but we heard Alice In Chains, Stone Temple Pilots and Smashing Pumpkins.

We were really bummed out, because we wanted a good, honest dose of good, honest metal and we got that instead. I mean, Stone Temple Pilots? What the hell's going on?

Mike D, September 1994

I like the way (Bis) move... I guess I like it that they're young and trying new stuff. And it's kinda inevitable with the music press, they build you up to knock you down. Well, now they're coming to America and once they sell a few records here it'll be fine again for another six months.

I first heard 'Kill Your Boyfriend', and then 'Kandy Pop' came out, but I thought it was cool when 'Fake DIY' was released because it showed the whole other side of Bis where they were actually making fun of all these people that were pursuing them. 'Tell It To The Kids' is great, too...

Mike D, March 1997, on Grand Royal signings Bis

I think they'll do really well in America. It's not like Britain, it's like a big wide country and it's a lot harder to get an immediate massive reaction. But just between my two trips to New York, everyone's talking about them so it's going to be that kind of route – as opposed to just putting out a single and playing again – people are already saying, "I just saw this amazing band." People recognise them walking around. Bis couldn't believe that people knew who they were.

Mike D, 1997

Amanda (from Bis) gave me a tape in Glasgow, pre-bidding war, and of course I wasn't, y'know, nearly smart enough to put it out then. I knew Gary Walker from Wiiija and – through Gary, I guess – they did those dates

opening up for Bikini Kill, and Bikini Kill came back and said, "We played with this band and basically we didn't think we were going to like them, because they're not politically motivated in any sense." They were really surprised they like Bis, y'know...

I always trust what others bands like, what my friends like, so I bought the records and the rest is history.

Mike D, March 1997

Run DMC's crossover hit with Aerosmith, 'Walk This Way', broke down a lot of barriers for us. Run DMC are coming from growing up in a black neighbourhood and being into black music and they're adding rock... We grew up with white music and we're putting rap into it. It's like we're coming from the opposite direction to them

Adam Y, December 1998

My favourite Peter Sellers movie is *The Party*, where he plays an Indian actor.

The movie was banned in India because he is playing this bumbling idiot in the middle of all these white people, and some Indian people were insulted by it. But the irony is that he's really the only intelligent person there – all the other people are morons. So it has a cool theme.

Adam Y (who registers at his hotel under the name I (Inspector) Clouseau), 1997

Pass The Mic
The Beasties From The Outside

Before the success I was big friends with Adrock, he spent one summer living in the same dorm as me and we'd hang out together all the time. And then when we became successful we'd still hang out but there'd be all these business managers and other people telling the other two I was trying to split the band.

It's success, suddenly there's so much pressure being applied to every situation by so many people. Also, people change.
Rick Rubin, July 1989

When (The Beastie Boys) first came to me they had on red shiny sweat suits and doo rags (bandannas). I put them in their own clothes again. They came to me talking about how *baaaad* they were. I didn't believe them, not because they were white but because they weren't **baaaad**!
Russell Simmons, June 1989

CBS asked us for another record, and we told them there was no more Beastie Boys because Yauch had asked Russell to manage his new band, Horovitz was out here seeing Molly (Ringwald) and was going to be a film star and Mike had his own band as well.

And so CBS said we couldn't have any more money because we weren't delivering what our contract required. So we explained this to The Beastie Boys and they just said, "F*** you". Also, Yauch felt he didn't like people thinking they were just puppets...
Rick Rubin, July 1989

I told them if you think there's something not cool about him (Mike D), we'll figure it out. There was

nothing cool about any of you when you came to me.
Russell Simmons, June 1989, on the Beasties' alleged original doubts about Mike

There were all kinds of things going on when they were breaking up, a lot of that was personal stuff between the band members. I would get phone calls from different band members saying, "I don't want to do this anymore, I hate that other guy, I can't picture myself doing this."
Rick Rubin, July 1989

To me, the Beasties are really like The Beatles. They're a band that started out with superficial music and grew and transformed into something different. They totally changed the music scene and our consciousness. That's what any Beatles comparison means to me. That's why I call them the Beastles.

The only reason people miss that is because the Beasties play hip-hop. Hip-hop is the music of today. If people don't understand that, they're either racist, stupid or blind.
Sean Lennon, September 1998

I first got into them when *Licensed To III* came out – one of the first tracks of theirs I heard was 'Paul Revere'. I wasn't so fond of 'Fight For Your Right To Party' because you'd go to parties and see really knobby people dancing to it.
Skint label boss Damien Harris, September 1998

It's just because we're white and we play hip-hop that we get compared to them. Anyway, we'd rather not discuss The Beastie Boys.
Stereo MCs, July 1989

I think they're a reference point for a lot of people. I really don't connect with them in that way, but then again I see the process, how it all goes together. I'm not really sure why they should have the effect on people that they do have.
Keyboardist Money Mark, September 1998

My relationship with them goes back to 'Cookie Puss' and the early Def Jam shows. Def Jam was the label that inspired me more than anything else. The Beastie Boys epitomised a brilliant assimilation of hip-hop by white people. No-one else could have done it. And with such humour. It's obvious they take their music seriously, but that's also about all they take seriously.
Wall Of Sound boss Mark Jones, September 1998

The Beastie Boys are still an influence on me. I actually met Tim (Goldsworthy, ex-partner at Mo'Wax) because he used to steal VW signs. I bought one off him. But the Beasties are very creative, clever and they have a spark, even after over a decade.
Mo'Wax boss James Lavelle, September 1998

Like all of us they're growing and learning and becoming wiser and richer as people. They have a great sense of humour. They're wild, wild, wild and crazy guys and it's nice that they are who they are – they have notoriety but they're also extremely down to earth.
  I think they use their fame in a constructive way. Which is very refreshing.
Jon Spencer Blues Explosion drummer Russell Simins, September 1998

Remember that no-one wanted to touch them for a while. They went from being credible to unfashionable and back to credible again. To survive all that is amazing. They've got a great spirit: they operate within their own world, regardless of anything else.
Wall Of Sound boss Mark Jones, September 1998

Since we toured we've evolved a very great friendship. Mike and I are mostly the ones who see each other. We hang out. We play basketball together.
I was a late bloomer when it came to hip-hop and rap. I knew Public Enemy and I dug it – living in New York City it was always around and was very exciting, but *Paul's Boutique* really drew me into it. I listened to that record so much I can't really listen to it anymore. I probably listen to *Check Your Head* the most.
Jon Spencer Blues Explosion drummer Russell Simins, September 1998

Yauch had started to put together the Tibet thing, so there was no time for working in the studio. We ended up not doing any recording for a year and then it was decided that they were going to do some recording in New York and we were gonna just take a few things with us, a lot smaller set-up.
  We went to Sean Lennon's rehearsal place for about a week and a half, just with an ADAT and minimal equipment. Adam Horovitz played all the instruments on 'Sneakin' Out The Hospital' – drums, bass and kalimba. The only things he didn't do on it were the percussion and the scratching. Everything was made from the demos and then we ended up adding stuff to it. Very rarely do we recreate it.
Mario Caldato, 1998, on the recording sessions for *Hello Nasty*

'Picture This' and 'Instant Death' were completely done at the Dungeon and, again, that's Adam Horovitz playing every instrument. He's basically a music lover. When he's at home, he had a hard time sleeping and he just works on music. You go to his house and he's just got records, disks, beatboxes, everything right there. 'Unite' was done with a loop from Dessau of a piano and then they added more stuff to it.
Mario Caldato, 1998

I met Mike more through Grand Royal than through The Beastie Boys. I'd wanted to work with them, and the guy that used to run Grand Royal also ran Mo'Wax in America for a while. Over the last few years Mike D has become a really good friend.

As far as the people who appear on the UNKLE record (*Psyence Fiction*) are concerned, I have a stronger relationship with Mike than anyone apart from Josh (Davis, alias DJ Shadow). He always wanted to do a track, but we had to wait until he'd sorted out his lyrics and finished with **Hello Nasty**.
Mo'Wax boss James Lavelle, September 1998

I was talking to Alex from the Propellerheads the other day. He said that *Paul's Boutique* was so revolutionary. Mostly for the way it mixed hip-hop with live instruments and the approach to the lyrics – it's a massive influence.

They're refreshing. It'd be easy for them to just sit around, but they'll only pack up if they stop having fun.
Wall Of Sound boss Mark Jones, September 1998

Check Your Head
Free Tibet, Buddhism And A New Way Of Thinking

I used to do interviews about the Tibetan situation completely separately from the band stuff, but I think it's okay to mix the two because the Tibetan people are very jovial even in the face of the oppression they are undergoing.
Adam Y, November 1997

The thing that's most significant about Tibet's struggle is that it's non-violent. Within Tibetan culture there are certain values of compassion and certain insights into how human beings need to treat each other in order to survive. So we need to focus not just on how to help Tibet, but also on what Tibet has to offer us…
We do these things having no idea how they're going to work. But then they all become this bigger undertaking as time goes on. I'm only just starting to get more comfortable talking about Tibet, especially the more the Tibetan people have thanked me. But everyone is in a position to affect the situation. Every individual through their purchasing power or voting power or letter-writing power has a tremendous effect.
Adam Y, January 1998

People say "How can you be politically active and put out the records you do and be kidding around all the time?" By saying that, you make something like politics unappealing to young people. It's a bunch of nonsense.
Mike D, September 1998

If you can imagine the stuff that these people have undergone, that your father has been imprisoned and tortured right now, or your mother has been sterilised, or you've been gang-raped, or whatever. If you can imagine the level of torture these people have undergone, and trying to maintain a level of total compassion toward the people that are doing this to them, and not have any anger or hatred toward them, it's hard…
Adam Y

Lately I've been learning about the situation in Tibet, and I can't get over what's going on there. I know that disgusting atrocities are going on all the time, all over the world, but for some reason this has grabbed a firm hold on my attention. Maybe it's because the Tibetan people are so peaceful and won't fight back even as the Chinese rape and torture them, prevent them from practising their religion and destroy their monasteries. (It's not unlike what America, the land of the free, has done to the Native Americans.)
Adam Y

I would not say drugs opened me up specifically to Buddhism. But when I first got interested in spirituality in '88 I was smoking a lot of herb and taking a lot of hallucinogens, and that starts to open you up. It removes your whole doubt system and opens up your chakras (centres of energy), and it becomes easy to start taking in a lot of information. Using drugs is a fairly uncontrolled way of approaching that stuff.
Adam Y, 1997

I'm not sure exactly what it is that grabbed hold of my attention… but my intention on writing about it here is clear. That the more people who become aware of the depth of

Tibetan culture, and the unimaginable human rights violations that are going on there, the sooner something will be done.

His Holiness the Dalai Lama has laid out an approach using economic sanctions, through which the Chinese would be forced to free Tibet. But at this point our country is far too greedy and self-centred for that.
Adam Y

This is one culture that's probably one of the most intelligent and advanced, mentally, in the world. So advanced that they won't act or take part in any violence, they won't defend themselves physically. And to allow them to be destroyed over money makes me embarrassed to be an American. It's just disgusting.
Adam Y

I figure, you know, conduct your life in ways that you feel are okay. There are the standards which are okay to other beings, and that includes the aliens.

Same way if you're trying not to have problems with other humans or yourself, then the same thing with the aliens. A lot of people have realised that people are trying to frame the aliens so they would have a miserable life.
Mike D, August 1998

Maybe seeing films of Tibetan monks and nuns (who have taken vows not to harm another living creature) being beaten in a public square was what got me. Or maybe it's that I've met so many of these people and see how happy they are, despite what's going on, laughing all the time without the same agenda of worries that so many of us carry in our modern society.

Or maybe it's that I see their society as an example of how people can live in peace working towards enlightenment. An example or blueprint of a way that a culture can operate in harmony with itself and the land. It's clear that if our world continues on its present course it will be destroyed and man extinct.
Adam Y

As Robert Thurman put it, the Tibetans are the example of 'inner modernity', that we need to contrast (with) our completely out of control, selfish, 'outer modernity'. With these two combined, we can balance out the powerful technological advances we've made with the wisdom to use them to do good. Tibet is in a sense a last hope. It is not so much that we should be so kind as to help these people for their sake alone, as that it is just as important to our own survival and that of the whole human race.
Adam Y

I first went to Nepal in 1990, than I took a second trip in December of 1992 and met some Tibetan people and started to learn about the oppression and what was going on. I stopped learning about the other religions and studied Buddhism for the next four to five years.
Adam Y

In terms of what I understand, Buddhism is like a manual to achieve enlightenment – there are these five things and these six things within the first thing, and all these little subdivisions. And, despite all of that right-brain information it is very heart-centred. At least that's the feeling I get.
Adam Y

Trying to do things that are positive is what brings a person true lasting happiness.
Adam Y, January 1998

I had been reading about a lot of different religions and spiritual paths and Native Americans for a while. What attracts me to Buddhism is the feeling I get from His Holiness the Dalai Lama and Tibetan people in general.

The people that I've met are really centred in the heart; they're coming from a real clear, compassionate place. And most of the teachings that I've read about almost seem set up to distract the other side of your brain in order to give your heart centre a chance to open up.
Adam Y

I haven't got anyone to give me a real solid definition of what a Buddhist is, so I kind of go back and forth. Sometimes I'll say I'm a Buddhist in interviews, and sometimes I'll say I'm not. I study life and people, and I think the Buddhist path is a really strong one, really intelligent.
Adam Y

The bottom line of all the problems on this planet and that all human beings are working on is this basic misconception of not-enoughness, feeling like we're not enough. This is some strain of that, of feeling that if the dharma is presented in this way, or if these other people become interested in this or get excited about it, it's going to take something away from me.
Adam Y, 1997

When I was a kid, I thought guns were really cool. I also liked fast cars and motorcycles. The way they're built, they're really attractive, the designs are really cool and they're loud. But when you start to think about it and realise that the primary intention of the thing is to harm other people, and you see how destructive they are, you gotta see beyond all the cool stuff.
Adam Y, August 1998

We were in Montana and there was a pawn shop and there was this really cool-looking gun, and I'd always wanted to get one. Then I started to get into Buddhism and I realised I had to get rid of it. I thought about taking it to the police, but if you turn it in it'll get recycled and then it still might wind up hurting somebody.

The optimal way of getting rid of it was to destroy it. So I went to Mario's (Beasties' producer) house 'cos he had a sledge hammer, I just went there to wreck it and he got his video camera out, and we ended up sticking it into the 'Something's Got To Give' video.
Adam Y, August 1998

It's not even enough to say we're not homophobic. You have to go the next step and say we're actually anti-homophobic and pro-gay. It makes me cringe if I think there's some guy with a Beastie Boys hat driving down the street saying, "Hey, f*** you, faggots!" That's not how we live our lives.
Mike D, 1994

It was suits. Not tuxedos or anything like that. It was a traditional Tibetan ceremony. This involved the bride travelling from her parents' house in the Upper East Side – where there was a ceremony to give her away – over to my parents' house in Brooklyn for the other half of the ceremony. My Dad made a little speech welcoming her.
Adam Y, September 1998, on his recent marriage

There was a time when we would joke around and say things that were disrespectful of women and think that it was funny, or that it wouldn't hurt anybody, or that it would be taken with a grain of salt. Then it became clear that that wasn't the case, and we had to go through the process of taking a step back and realising how

those things affect other people.
The lyric in 'Sure Shot' is just a statement of that. It's just seeing things from a different perspective…
Adam Y, 1997, on the attitude towards women expressed in some of the band's early songs

Even on the last album (*III Communication*) there aren't any lyrics that are disrespectful of women, but we went an extra step on this album to make a statement. Mainly where it's coming from is that I listen to a lot of hip-hop, and there is so much disrespect for women that it's become standardised, normal.
It's like a blemish in a good song. You hear a good record, all of a sudden there'll be some obnoxious lyrics in there.
Adam Y, 1997

I don't think the industry ever thought of us as more than a novelty. We were viewed as humorous without anything of length to offer.
Mike D

This year definitely seems like a blur. And it almost seems like two years, because the first half of the year was spent while we were still working on the record, probably on the part of the record where we were working most intensely 'cos it was the very end and we had these deadlines that we imposed on ourselves.
So we were working a lot of hours and a lot of days and focusing a lot of attention on just trying to finish the record. And then that got gone and we immediately dove head first into everything else after it…
Mike D, December 1998

People ask us "Hasn't it been a great year for the band?" And to me my life just continues. And it's not that significantly different whether the band is or is not very much in the public eye. Y'know, I hang out with

friends. I have a life separate to the band, and I always have done.
Adam Y, December 1998

We've realised this year playing live that this is what we actually do. Making records and playing shows. It might sound corny, but it's the crux of what we do.
Mike D, December 1998

When you take our most extreme points and put them next to one

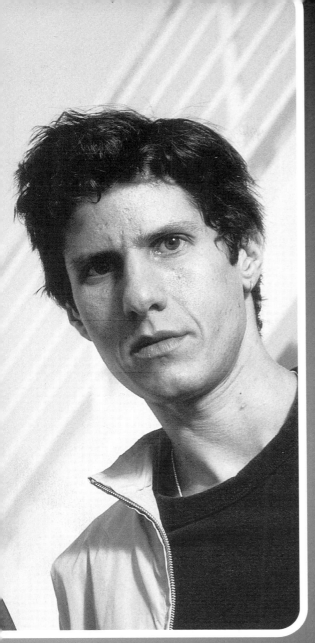

cool, I've got a gun too" it makes you re-think about how what you do is affecting others.
Adam Y, November 1997

As you evolve you become more aware of things. It's an ongoing process of having your eyes opened.
Mike D, November 1997

I'm pretty hopeful about the evolution of humanity in general. I think that all of us here on the planet at this point have come into these lifetimes and into these bodies because it's a crucial time in the evolution of the planet and humanity. It's a transitional phase, and I think that everyone has come in at this time to be a part of that, to be part of the Big Show.
Adam Y, 1997

The only moment you ever have on your own in your entire life is when you're shitting. Some guys love to shit in front of their buddies.
Mike D, July 1989

(One) approach to finance is completely avoiding it, as in learning to live on no money. As far as I'm concerned, this is the ultimate solution: to survive without currency and be happy.
   I spent a few years in the no-money cycle, and it has its virtues – it frees you from the agonising humiliations that jobs can inspire. However, society at large views those without dough as relatively worthless, and you're kind of limited in terms of what you can do when it comes to entertainment, sleeping arrangements, eating and transportation.
Mike D

If you don't have the patience or disposition for indentured servitude or the no-money lifestyle, I advise you to go the entrepreneurial route.
Mike D

another it does sound pretty far-fetched, but we've changed a lot since (1987). That stuff was all in good fun, but we realised that some of those things were either embarrassing to ourselves or destructive to others.
   It was the same when we sang about violence on the records, from the sense that we thought cowboy movies were funny. But when you get kids coming up to you at concerts going, "Hey you guys are